ON THE COSMIC MYSTERY OF JESUS CHRIST

ST VLADIMIR'S SEMINARY PRESS
Popular Patristics Series
Number 25

The Popular Patristics Series published by St Vladimir's Seminary Press provides readable and accurate translations of a broad range of early Christian literature to a wide audience—from students of Christian history to lay Christians reading for spiritual benefit. Recognized scholars in their fields provide short but comprehensive and clear introductions to the material. The texts include classics of Christian literature, thematic volumes, collections of homilies, letters on spiritual counsel, and poetical works from a variety of geographical contexts and historical backgrounds. The mission of the series is to mine the riches of the early Church and to make these treasures available to all.

Series Editor
JOHN BEHR

On the *Cosmic Mystery* of *Jesus Christ*

Selected *Writings* from

ST MAXIMUS THE CONFESSOR

Translated by

PAUL M. BLOWERS

and

ROBERT LOUIS WILKEN

ST VLADIMIR'S SEMINARY PRESS
CRESTWOOD, NEW YORK 10707

Library of Congress Cataloging-in-Publication Data

Maximus, Confessor, Saint, ca. 580–662.
    [Selections. English. 2003]
    On the cosmic mystery of Jesus Christ : selected writings from St. Maximus the Confessor / translated by Paul M. Blowers and Robert Louis Wilken.
        p.   cm. — (St. Vladimir's Seminary Press "popular patristics" series)
    Includes bibliographical references.
    ISBN 0–88141–249–x
    ISSN 1555–5755
    1. Jesus Christ—History of doctrines—Middle Ages, 600–1500.   I. Blowers, Paul M., 1955–   I. Wilken, Robert Louis, 1936–   III. Title.   IV. Series.

BR65.M412E5 2003
232—dc21

2002037184

ISBN 0–88141–249–x
ISBN 978–0–88141–249–9
ISSN 1555–5755

The Pulley (1633)

by George Herbert

When God at first made man,
Having a glass of blessings standing by;
Let us (said he) pour on him all we can;
Let the world's riches, which dispersed lie,
　　Contract into a span.

So strength first made a way;
Then beauty flowed, then wisdom, honour,
　　pleasure:
When almost all was out, God made a stay,
Perceiving that alone of all his treasure
　　Rest in the bottom lay.

For if I should (said he)
Bestow this jewel also on my creature,
He would adore my gifts instead of me,
And rest in Nature, not the God of Nature;
　　So both should losers be.

Yet let him keep the rest,
But keep them with repining restlessness:
Let him be rich and weary, that at least,
If goodness lead him not, yet weariness
　　May toss him to my breast

Table of Contents

THE TEXTS

Preface

This translation from its inception has been a collaborative effort, motivated by the need for published translations of the writings of St Maximus the Confessor. Robert Wilken provided the translation and notes for the crucially important text of *Ambiguum 7*. Paul Blowers translated and annotated all the other texts in this volume, and wrote the Introduction. Yet both translators have profited from mutual sharing of ideas on the rendering of specific passages in the texts presented here.

Translating Maximus's sophisticated Greek into English, and especially into a contemporary idiom, is a challenging process. Maximus himself was meticulous in his use of language, and given to continuous qualification and clarification of his own discourse. His literary legacy bids his readers and translators to exercise the same scruples. The goal of this translation has been readability, but not at the cost of oversimplifying Maximus's richly textured language and style. The Confessor's discourses are full of important terms drawn from the earlier conciliar tradition, other terms derived from the rich spiritual vocabulary of his monastic heritage, and still other "keywords" expressing very precise nuances in his theological vision. At many points in the translation, therefore, specific Greek terms or phrases have been included in parentheses or in the notes to highlight significant shades of meaning; and the translators have frequently commented on specific terms and phrases and their background both in Maximus and the larger patristic tradition. One very important example is Maximus's terminology of human volition, including his well-developed distinction between stable willing (θέλησις), rooted in nature, and the deliberative "gnomic" will (γνώμη) stunted by the fall. Such a distinction can all too easily be lost in translation. Indeed, it is difficult to find the terms in English to convey what Maximus and other ancient writers understood to be a whole elaborate process of willing and acting.

Two major editions of Maximus's writings have been used in this translation. For the *Ambigua* and the theological *Opuscula*, the only Greek text currently available is that of J.-P. Migne's *Patrologia Graeca* (vol. 91), to which reference is made by column number(s) and section(s). The translations from the *Quaestiones ad Thalassium* are based on the excellent two-volume critical edition by Carl Laga and Carlos Steel in the *Corpus Christianorum, series graeca* (vols. 7 and 22), and here the references are made to volume number, page(s), and line(s). Critical editions of other patristic works are similarly cited by volume number in the series, columns or pages, and sections or lines.

Production of this translation of St Maximus owes much to the encouragement, friendship, and critical eye of Professor John Behr of St Vladimir's Orthodox Theological Seminary. It is hoped that this translation, of one of the greatest theologians of the Orthodox tradition, will be a welcome addition to the "Popular Patristics" series of St Vladimir's Seminary Press.

Paul M. Blowers
Emmanuel School of Religion
Johnson City, Tennessee

Robert Louis Wilken
University of Virginia
Charlottesville, Virginia

Abbreviations

ACW   Ancient Christian Writers (ed. J. Quasten et al.)

CCSG   Corpus Christianorum, Series Graeca

CWS   Classics of Western Spirituality

GCS   Griechischen christlichen Schriftsteller der ersten drei Jahrhunderte

GNO   Gregorii Nysseni Opera (ed. W. Jaeger et al.)

PG   Patrologia Graeca (ed. J.-P. Migne)

PL   Patrologia Latina (ed. J.-P. Migne)

Introduction

Maximus the Confessor (580–662) lived, historically and to some extent geographically, betwixt and between. Historically, he lived in the indefinite transition between "early" and "medieval" Christianity: after the downfall of the Western Roman Empire and the zenith of the Byzantine Christian Empire under Justinian, but before the schism of Byzantine and Roman Churches had reached the point of no return; after the crucial Councils of Nicea (325), Constantinople (381), and Chalcedon (451), but before the age of the Ecumenical Councils had ended; after the most creative epoch in patristic thought, stretching from Origen to the Cappadocian Fathers and Augustine, but before the tendency toward theological scholasticism East or West had fully gained momentum.[1]

Even geographically, Maximus lived part of his life on a virtual frontier between East and West. According to the traditional Greek *Life* of Maximus, he was raised in Constantinople, received an appointment in the imperial court, but soon left it to become a monk.[2] After spending his early monastic career in Asia Minor, he may have traveled to points East before moving to North Africa, where he came under the spiritual direction of Sophronius, the

---

[1] For a general portrait of Maximus and his achievement, see Paul M. Blowers, "Theology as Visionary, Integrative, Pastoral: The Legacy of Maximus the Confessor," *Pro Ecclesia* 2 (1993): 216–30.

[2] The traditional Greek *Life* of Maximus, dating to the tenth century, may be found in PG 90:68–108. There is also a controversial Syriac *Life* of Maximus, which gives an alternative account of his birth and monastic formation. Composed by a Monothelite biographer whose bias against Maximus is obvious, this account has him a native of Palestine, of a tainted family background, and trained early on in an

future bishop of Jerusalem who had a formative influence on Maximus's Christology and his response to emerging Monothelitism. Sophronius was most likely the abbot of Maximus's monastic community, the Eukratas monastery near Carthage, which provided safe haven for refugee Eastern monks in the wake of the Arab invasions.[3]

The dearth of sources restricts our knowledge of North Africa in the period preceding Maximus's arrival. Yet evidence suggests that the older Roman Christian culture of Augustine's time had all but disappeared. Donatism, the indigenous ecclesiastical movement that had once posed a severe challenge to Augustine's church, was also in retreat. African Catholics seem initially to have praised the Byzantine reconquest in the sixth century for lifting the Vandal (and Arian) yoke, but they quickly grew disenchanted with Justinian's enforcement of doctrinal reforms on them, particularly his condemnation of the Three Chapters. This and other imperial initiatives, such as the public campaign to reinforce the cult of the Theotokos, aimed at appeasing the Monophysite churches of the East, and were largely irrelevant to the Africans.[4]

In the seventh century, the rapid immigration of Byzantine

Origenist monastery. See Sebastian Brock, "An Early Syriac Life of Maximus the Confessor," *Analecta Bollandiana* 91 (1975): 299–346.

[3]For the documentation of Maximus's biography, see Pauline Allen and Bronwen Neil, eds., *Documenta ad vitam sancti Maximi Confessoris spectantia*, CCSG (Leuven: Brepols, forthcoming). Still exceedingly useful is the study of Polycarp Sherwood, *An Annotated Date-List of the Works of Maximus the Confessor*, Studia anselmiana 30 (Rome: Herder, 1952), especially pp. 1–22. For good concise summaries of Maximus's life and some of the reconstructive problems it poses, see Jean-Claude Larchet, *La divinisation de l'homme selon saint Maxime le Confesseur*, Cogitatio fidei 194 (Paris: Les Éditions du Cerf, 1996), pp. 7–20; Andrew *Louth, Maximus the Confessor*, The Early Church Fathers (London and New York: Routledge, 1996), pp. 3–18; and Lars Thunberg, *Microcosm and Mediator: The Theological Anthropology of Maximus the Confessor*, 2nd ed. (Chicago: Open Court Publishing, 1995), pp. 1–7.

[4]For a detailed examination of these developments, see Averil Cameron, "Byzantine Africa: The Literary Evidence," in *Excavations at Carthage 1978*, ed. J. H. Humphreys (Ann Arbor: University of Michigan Press, 1982), pp. 32–8; reprinted in her collected essays, *Changing Cultures in Early Byzantium*, Variorum Collected Studies Series 536 (Aldershot, U.K. and Brookfield, Vt.: Ashgate Publishing, 1996).

refugee monks—and especially Sophronius and Maximus—signaled a crucial turning point. As Averil Cameron puts it, "their arrival was a tonic."[5] They would now help rally the African church against the latest imperial imposition: Monotheletism. In 645, approximately fifteen years after he came to Carthage, Maximus defeated the Monothelite ex-patriarch Pyrrhus in public debate and drew immediate support from the African bishops, while the Byzantine exarch Gregory, who had been present at the debate, actually initiated an open rebellion against Constantinople in a failed bid for African independence. Maximus's participation in the Lateran Council in Rome in 649 allied him and his African following with the papacy and set the stage for a final showdown with the imperial authorities in the latter's crusade toward Monothelite conformity.[6]

By a sad irony, when at last he returned to his native Constantinople, Maximus, along with Pope Martin I, was in imperial custody, an enemy of the state. He was put on trial in 655,[7] exiled, cross-examined, exiled again, tried again, publicly mutilated, exiled yet once more, and died still under disgrace in 662 at the fortress of Schemaris in Lazica, a region on the eastern shore of the Black Sea (in contemporary Georgia).[8] These heroic tribulations, for which Maximus earned his epithet "the Confessor," proved nevertheless to be the refiner's fire of the Dyothelite orthodoxy vindicated in the

[5]Ibid., p. 41.

[6]Ibid., pp. 38–51, and especially pp. 44–45. See also John Haldon, *Byzantium in the Seventh Century: The Transformation of a Culture* (Cambridge: Cambridge University Press, 1990), pp. 304–13.

[7]The record of this first trial, the *Relatio Motionis*, traditionally attributed to one of Maximus's two close disciples, either Anastasius the Apocrisarius or Anastasius the Monk, can be found in Pauline Allen and Bronwen Neil, eds., *Scripta saeculi VII vitam Maximi Confessoris illustrantia*, CCSG 39 (Turnhout: Brepols, 1999), pp. 14–51; English translation of this and related documents from Maximus's exiles are provided by Allen and Neil in *Maximus the Confessor and His Companions: Documents from Exile*, Oxford Early Christian Texts (Oxford: Oxford University Press, 2002). See also the English trans. of the first trial by George Berthold in *Maximus Confessor: Selected Writings*, Classics of Western Spirituality (Mahwah, N.J.: Paulist Press, 1985), pp. 15–31.

[8]For the further documentation of these events at the close of Maximus's life, see Allen and Neil, eds., *Scripta saeculi VII vitam Maximi Confessoris illustrantia*.

Sixth Ecumenical Council at Constantinople in 681. Though his
name was not acknowledged in the official documents of the Council, recognition of St Maximus the Confessor's decisive work in the
shaping of Eastern Orthodoxy, and of his mediatorial role as one of
the few genuinely ecumenical theologians of the patristic era, was
assured.[9]

MAXIMUS, THEOLOGIAN OF
THE TRANSFIGURED COSMOS

Georges Florovsky quite appropriately described the theological
achievement of Maximus the Confessor in terms of a grand "sym-
phony of experience" rather than a perfectly contoured and self-
enclosed doctrinal system.[10] More recently Cyril O'Regan, again
using the analogy of a "symphonic" theology, has suggested that
Maximus's work is an extended and richly textured gloss on the
Chalcedonian Definition, which functions for him as "a dense knot
of implication, both visionary and interpretive," that holds the mys-
terious key to the world and its salvation.[11] To be sure, Maximus's
theological reasoning at times comes to expression in an exacting
logic and use of syllogisms; and he is often meticulously precise in
the nuances of his theological language. Yet all the while *theologia*—
as the aspiration to intimate knowledge of the Holy Trinity that
must always remain grounded in, and integrated with, the contem-
plative and ascetic life of the Christian—entails for this Byzantine
sage an intensive, ongoing, multifaceted "intellectual quest" (ἐξέτα-

[9]See Jean-Claude Larchet, *Maxime le Confesseur, médiateur entre l'Orient et
l'Occident*, Cogitatio Fidei 208 (Paris: Les Éditions du Cerf, 1998); also Andrew Louth,
"St. Maximus the Confessor: Between East and West," *Studia Patristica* 32, ed. Elizabeth Livingstone (Leuven: Peeters Press, 1997), pp. 332–45.

[10]See Georges Florovsky, *The Byzantine Fathers of the Sixth to Eighth Century*,
Collected Works of Georges Florovsky 10, trans. Raymond Miller et al. (Vaduz: Büchervertriebsanstalt, 1987), p. 213.

[11]Cyril O'Regan, "Von Balthasar and Thick Retrieval: Post-Chalcedonian Symphonic Theology," *Gregorianum* 77 (1996): 246–7.

σις) into the foundations and future of the world created by God, recreated through the work of Jesus Christ, sanctified by the Holy Spirit, and summoned to an unprecedented and glorious deifica-tion.[12] "Questing after" this grand mystery, as Maximus indicates in *Ad Thalassium* 59 on 1 Peter 1:10–11, was the labor of the ancient prophets, from Abraham to Zechariah, and now is the vocation of every Christian whose natural intellectual and moral faculties are continually being stretched by the grace of the Holy Spirit.[13]

Maximus has been called a *cosmic* theologian, and rightly so.[14] For Maximus the Confessor, the world—the natural world and the "world" of the scriptural revelation—is the broad and complex the-ater in which God's incarnational mission is playing itself out to full completion.[15] Both the cosmos and the Bible tell the same glorious story, as it were: the story of the Logos who, in his historical incar-nation and in his gradual eschatological epiphany "in all things" (cf 1 Cor 15:28), discloses through the *logoi*, the providential "principles" of creation and Scripture, the magnificent intricacy and beauty of the transfigured cosmos.[16] At the center of this cosmic drama, the true play-within-the-play, is the hypostatic union of divine and human natures and wills that is not only operative "in" Jesus Christ but which truly *is* Jesus Christ. Maximus's cosmic and christocentric vision, however, comes down to us not in any finalized *summa*, but in carefully worked out insights—relatively brief ones at that—

[12]On this theme in Maximus's theological method, see Vittorio Croce, *Tradizione e ricerca: Il metodo teologico di san Massimo il Confessore*, Studia patristica mediola-nensia 2 (Milan: Vita e Pensiero, 1974).

[13]*Ad Thalassium* 59 (CCSG 22:45, 12–51, 116).

[14]See, in particular, Lars Thunberg's two definitive works, *Microcosm and Medi-ator* (note 3 above) and *Man and the Cosmos: The Vision of St Maximus the Confessor* (Crestwood, N.Y.: St Vladimir's Seminary Press, 1985); also David Yeago, "Jesus of Nazareth and Cosmic Redemption: The Relevance of St. Maximus the Confessor," *Modern Theology* 12 (1996): 163–93; Louth, *Maximus the Confessor*, pp. 63–77; John Meyendorff, "The Cosmic Dimension of Salvation," ch. 7 in his *Christ in Eastern Christian Thought* (Crestwood, N.Y.: St Vladimir's Seminary Press, 1975), pp. 131–51.

[15]Thus Maximus's celebrated phrase that the divine Logos "wills always and in all things to accomplish the mystery of his embodiment" (*Amb.* 7, PG 91:1084C–D).

[16]See especially *Amb.* 10 (PG 91:1125D–1129D).

spread across his writings mostly in the form of scholia (extended elucidations either of patristic authorities or of problematic texts of Scripture), epistles, theological mini-commentaries (*opuscula*), spiritual "chapters" (*kephalaia*); but also in a trenchant commentary on the Divine Liturgy, his *Mystagogia,* cherished by historians of the Byzantine rite, and in a deeply mystagogical *Commentary on the Lord's Prayer.*[17]

The cosmic scope of Maximus's theology has been analyzed from a wide variety of perspectives. From a cultural-historical standpoint, for example, Averil Cameron has drawn attention to the dramatic transitions and cultural insecurities of Maximus's own time. In her view, Maximus, like John Damascene later on, was concerned to "define the limits of the safe Christian world," a stable Hellenic Christian culture, by developing a thorough systematization of Christian knowledge that could secure Christian identity in the era of heresy and invasion following the reign of Justinian.[18] Maximus, like other writers of his age, contributed to the formation of "a discourse that provided for a secure sense of total order, the perception that all knowledge could be contained in one system embracing all things human and divine."[19] Cameron's reconstruction is compelling, and identifies a process of which Maximus himself, who

[17]See Sherwood, *An Annotated Date-List of the Works of Maximus the Confessor,* pp. 23–56. On the genre of Maximus's works see also Paul M. Blowers, *Exegesis and Spiritual Pedagogy in Maximus the Confessor: An Investigation of the Quaestiones ad Thalassium,* Christianity and Judaism in Antiquity 7 (Notre Dame, Ind.: University of Notre Dame Press, 1991), pp. 28–94.

[18]Averil Cameron, "Disputations, Polemical Literature and the Formation of Opinion in the Early Byzantine Period," in *Dispute Poems and Dialogues in the Ancient and Mediaeval Near East,* ed G. J. Reinink and H. L. J. Vanstiphout, Orientalia lovaniensia analecta 42 (Leiden: Brill, 1991), pp. 100–2, 106–7; reprinted in *Changing Cultures in Early Byzantium.* On the process of cultural transition and transformation in Maximus's time, see also Haldon, *Byzantium in the Seventh Century,* especially pp. 436–58.

[19]Averil Cameron, "Byzantium and the Past in the Seventh Century: The Search for Redefinition," in *The Seventh Century: Change and Continuity,* ed. J. Fontaine and J. N. Hillgarth (London: Wartburg Institute, 1992), pp. 268–71; reprinted in *Changing Cultures in Early Byzantium.*

makes few explicit references to the politics and culture of his time, may not have been directly conscious. We must constantly keep in mind that his theological vision did not simply aspire to a transcendent, timeless contemplation of the world, but also addressed the concrete context of a culture still undergoing redefinition, a culture rocked by the emergence of a whole new religious and political entity on its immediate horizon: Islam.[20] Yet Cameron's observations on Maximus's discourse must be qualified by duly considering the Confessor's own profound sense of the limitedness of human comprehension—our "stumbling and staggering"—in the quest of spiritual truth,[21] and by his insistence on an ongoing theological quest that resists facile systematization, as noted above.

From a philosophical-theological standpoint, as Polycarp Sherwood and others have demonstrated, Maximus's cosmic theology constitutes a fundamental correction of the "system" of Origenism that remained an object of devotion within certain Eastern monastic communities long after its formal condemnation at the Council of Constantinople in 553.[22] By this account, Maximus appears both as beneficiary and expander of the critical treatment of Origenism that the Cappadocian Fathers, especially Gregory of Nyssa, had already undertaken three centuries earlier.

Hans Urs von Balthasar, honoring the achievement of Sherwood, concentrated even more attention on the christocentric core of Maximus's cosmic theology, and insisted on the centrality of the Chalcedonian Definition in the Confessor's cosmological synthesis.[23] Lars Thunberg's important work on Maximus, in turn, has built on the

[20]Maximus in fact briefly refers to the Arab onslaught in his *Epistle* 14 (PG 91:540A).
[21]*Amb.* 10 (PG 91:1160B).
[22]Polycarp Sherwood, *The Earlier Ambigua of St. Maximus the Confessor and His Refutation of Origenism*, Studia anselmiana 36 (Rome: Herder, 1955); also Irénée-Henri Dalmais, "Saint Maxime Confesseur et la crise de l'origénisme monastique," in *Théologie de la vie monastique: études sur la tradition patristique*, Théologie 49 (Paris: Aubier, 1961), pp. 411–21.
[23]Hans Urs von Balthasar, *Kosmische Liturgie: Das Weltbild Maximus' des Bekenners*, 2nd ed. (Einsiedeln: Johannes-Verlag, 1961); cf O'Regan, "Von Balthasar and Thick Retrieval," pp. 227–60.

labors of both Sherwood and von Balthasar but moved deeper into the intricacies of Maximus's developing spiritual vision of the universe, with the mystery of Christ and creaturely deification as the key to comprehending the whole panorama. As Thunberg puts it,

> It is rather his visionary understanding of the Person of Christ which is most important, not only for [Maximus] himself but for the evaluation of his role. The hypostatic relationship between human and divine in Christ, as he understands it in his personal faithfulness to both Chalcedon and Constantinople, is alone able to manifest and safeguard the purpose for which man was created, deification, while preserving man himself unchanged in his natural make-up. It alone establishes man in an unchangeable union with God forever, if only he is willing, by divine grace, to receive the deifying powers as effective within himself.[24]

In Maximus's vision of the world, the incarnation of the Second Person of the Holy Trinity in Jesus of Nazareth holds the secret to the foundations—the architectural *logoi*—of the created cosmos,[25] its destiny after the fall of created beings (the mystery of *redemption*), and the transcendent end (τέλος) of creation (the mystery of *deification*) wherein the prospect of ever more intimate communion with the Trinity is opened up.[26] Maximus's achievement, from one angle, is a panoramic commentary on the first chapter of Ephesians and on Colossians 1:15–23, the Apostle Paul's reflections on the mystery of Christ as the mystery of the world. Though filtered through a mature trinitarian theology and Christology in which he shows his

[24]Thunberg, *Microcosm and Mediator*, p. 433.
[25]On the philosophical foundations of Maximus's christocentric ontology, see Torstein Tollefsen, *The Christocentric Cosmology of St. Maximus the Confessor: A Study of His Metaphysical Principles*, Acta Humaniora 72 (Oslo: Unipub Forlag, 2000).
[26]Thus Maximus's celebrated statement in his *Commentary on the Lord's Prayer* (CCSG 23:31, 87–89): "In becoming incarnate the Logos of God instructs us in *theologia*, since he shows in himself the Father and the Holy Spirit."

debt to the Cappadocian Fathers, we see in Maximus's achievement the echoes of Irenaeus's principle of cosmic *recapitulation* (ἀνα-κεφαλαίωσις),[27] and a critical rehabilitation of Origen's masterful insight into the divine penetration and permeation of all things (1 Cor 15:28). In his various "incarnations"—in the *logoi* of the world, in the spiritual meanings (*logoi*) of Scripture, supremely in Jesus Christ, and ultimately in the virtuous life of the faithful[28]—the Logos is the supreme divine Mediator, while humanity, the microcosm of the created order, and bearer of the divine image, enjoys the graced vocation of participation in Christ's mediation. Maximus develops this correlation most poignantly in *Ambiguum* 41 and *Ad Thalassium* 48.[29] Christ, through his ministry of incarnation, death, resurrection, and ascension, has overcome both the natural and the unnatural (postlapsarian) divisions within creation; likewise humanity shares in his ministry of cosmic reconciliation (or "reintegration," as Thunberg calls it) through the multifaceted disciplines of ascetic practice (πρᾶξις), contemplation (θεωρία), and elevated mystical insight (θεολογία).

TEXTS AND THEMES

The present volume includes representative texts from Maximus's corpus which have heretofore not appeared in a published English translation. They provide the reader with a relatively comprehen-

[27]See especially *Ad Thal.* 60 translated below.

[28]The notion of the multiple "incarnations" of the Logos, inspired originally by Origen, also bespeaks Maximus's understanding of the sacramental character of revelation; it is divine *embodiment* in its fullness (cf *Amb.* 7, PG 91:1084C–D; *Amb.* 33, 1285C–1288A). On this notion, see Thunberg, *Microcosm and Mediator*, pp. 77–9, 323–30; Blowers, *Exegesis and Spiritual Pedagogy in Maximus the Confessor*, pp. 119–22.

[29]*Amb.* 41 (PG 91:1309A–1312B), Eng. trans. in Louth, *Maximus the Confessor*, pp. 159–60; *Ad Thal.* 48 (CCSG 7:333, 65–335, 81). See also Panayiotis Nellas, *Deification in Christ: Orthodox Perspectives on the Nature of the Human Person* (Crestwood, N.Y.: St Vladimir's Seminary Press, 1987), pp. 211–18. On the various aspects of humanity's mediatorial role, see Thunberg's extensive discussion in *Microcosm and Mediator*, pp. 331–427.

sive, though by no means exhaustive, portrait of some preeminent themes in his cosmic theology and spirituality. Most of the texts come from Maximus's two largest works, the *Ambigua* and the *Quaestiones ad Thalassium*.[30]

The Latin term *ambiguum* is a rendition of the Greek *aporia*, "difficulty" or "problem," and Maximus's *Ambigua* are similar to works that go under the name *Quaestiones et Responsa*, questions and answers. The earlier *Ambigua* (nos. 6–71, dating ca. 628–30) seem to have arisen from conversations between Maximus and John, bishop of Cyzicus in Asia Minor. Most of the topics discussed in these *Ambigua* have to do with questions about passages from the writings of Gregory the Theologian, bishop of Nazianzus in the fourth century. Gregory was a revered teacher, the first Christian thinker since St John the Evangelist to be granted the honorary title "the Theologian"[31] (the only other thereafter being Symeon the New Theologian in the early eleventh century). In the sixth century, however, followers of Origen of Alexandria appealed to the writings of Gregory in support of their teachings. In writing the *Ambigua* Maximus wished to show that passages used by the Origenists did not support their views and could be, indeed must be, understood in an orthodox way.

The *Ad Thalassium*, dating slightly later (ca. 630–33), consists in Maximus's responses to queries on scriptural *aporiae* sent to him by his Libyan friend, "the presbyter and hegumen" Thalassius, most likely for the benefit of Thalassius's whole community of monks.[32] A number of the questions take up exegetical problems raised in earlier patristic exegesis, while others clearly reflect the monks' con-

[30]*Quaestiones ad Thalassium* is the traditional title, but the actual Greek title is better rendered *To Thalassius, Most Holy Presbyter and Hegumen, Concerning Diverse Difficulties from Holy Scripture.*

[31]See John McGuckin, *Saint Gregory of Nazianzus: An Intellectual Biography* (Crestwood, N.Y.: St Vladimir's Seminary Press, 2001).

[32]On the context and genre of the *Ad Thalassium*, see Blowers, *Exegesis and Spiritual Pedagogy in Maximus the Confessor*, pp. 2–94. Thalassius himself proved to be a spiritual writer of serious repute, as evidenced by his inclusion in the *Philokalia*.

cerns to garner spiritual riches from discrepant or obscure biblical texts. In the *Ad Thalassium,* Maximus reveals his debt to the Alexandrian hermeneutical tradition, including the principle that the Holy Spirit has inserted "obstacles" (σκάνδαλα) in Scripture to prompt us to explore its deeper mysteries. Maximus demonstrates as well his keen ability to develop spiritual doctrine from the multiple senses of the scriptural text. His responses are at once deeply theological and practical.

One last text (*Opusculum* 6) comes from Maximus's *Opuscula theologica et polemica* ("Short Theological and Polemical Works"), which span his entire career and probe a number of theological issues and definitions arising from the doctrinal controversies of his time. Of particular interest are the christological *Opuscula* (*Opusc.* 6 among them) which Maximus composed specifically to counteract Monotheletism and to define ever more precisely his doctrine of the two wills of Jesus Christ.

Cosmic "First Principles"

Ad Thalassium 2, though brief, provides a splendid encapsulation of the cosmological foundations of Maximus's theology. In it we find a portrait of the *logoi* of creation grounding the Creator's will for the world and the process by which the movements and actions of individual creatures are to be integrated toward the universal "principle of rational being," which is none other than the divine plan for deifying the cosmos. And yet no text from Maximus's writings affords us a more comprehensive philosophical perspective on his cosmology and eschatology than *Ambiguum* 7. It is the most learned and trenchant criticism of Origen's cosmological views and an early statement of Maximus's teaching on creation and fall, body and soul, and the final end of human life. Hans Urs von Balthasar calls it the "single most significant anti-Origenist writing from Greek patristic literature."[33]

In *Oration* 14 Gregory the Theologian had written that "we who

---

[33] *Kosmische Liturgie,* p. 123. See also Sherwood, *The Earlier Ambigua,* pp. 21–9, 72–102.

24

I have slipped down from above." The Origenists
mean that before the world came into existence
: connatural with God and had their dwelling in
__ a state of perpetual rest contemplating God. But
over time out of satiety (κόρος) they grew weary of contemplating
God and they fell away from God into bodies, "slipped down" in the
words of Gregory's oration. This "fall" led God to create the world
so that souls might be led back to the unity they once enjoyed by a
long process of education.

In *Ambiguum* 7 Maximus shows that these views have no basis
in Gregory's writings and presents his own views on how the world
came to be and on the final end of all things. For the Origenists pre-
existent souls, who had "cooled off," moved away from an initial
unity with God; for Maximus, human beings, who in a historical fall
abused their freedom to turn toward what was worse, in Christ are
able to move toward God who draws them by grace into his diviniz-
ing life. The argument turns on the understanding of movement.
For Origen the basic scheme was rest (στάσις) in God followed by
movement (κίνησις) away from God that led to "becoming" (γένεσις), the coming into being of things, i.e. the creation of the world.
Maximus argues that his view cannot withstand philosophical
scrutiny. For it assumes that God, who is supremely beautiful and
ultimately desirable, is incapable of satisfying the desire of those
who seek God. If rational beings had in fact reached the "end," that
is, rest in God, and were moved to turn away from God, what will
prevent this from happening again and again. "What could be
greater reason to despair?" asks Maximus.[34]

In response Maximus turns Origen's scheme on its head. Instead
of "rest," "movement" and "becoming" (coming to be), he proposes
"becoming" followed by "movement" that has as its goal "rest."
Movement in Maximus's view is understood positively as movement
toward the Good, that is, toward God. His term for the end, "rest," is
drawn from biblical verses such as Deuteronomy 12:9 and Hebrews

[34]*Amb.* 7 (PG 91:1069C).

4:10. Rest is the goal, the end toward which we move, the fulfillment of our yearnings. When the end is reached one no longer wants anything of one's own and delights in being wholly embraced by God. "Nothing besides God will be known, nor will there be anything opposed to God that could entice one to desire it . . . It is like light from the stars. The stars do not shine in the day. When the greater and incomparable light of the sun appears, they are hidden and cannot be seen by the senses."[35]

Though Maximus uses a technical vocabulary and the arguments of the treatise move on a very sophisticated philosophical plane his language is permeated with biblical words and he rests his discussion on key biblical texts. In the early part of the treatise he cites a number of biblical texts that speak of the incompleteness of the present and of the glory that will be revealed at the end of time; for example: "I will be satisfied when your glory appears"(Ps 16:15).[36] And toward the end he cites passages from St Paul on the mystery hidden before the ages (Col 1:26) now revealed in Christ that anticipates the consummation of all things at the end of time. His point is that the transformation that God brings about "did not come through the normal course of things." It was only realized when God "joined himself to us" and a "new way of being human appeared,"[37] the person of Christ, true God and true man.

Finally, Maximus has an interesting discussion of the unity of body and soul in human beings, a matter of some importance since it was through the flesh of Christ that God renewed fallen human beings.[38] It is foolish to think, as the Origenists claim, that souls existed before bodies. Body and soul are parts of man and as parts each necessarily has a relation to the other. Even the body, after sep-

[35]*Amb.* 7 (1077A).
[36]*Amb.* 7 (1072D–1073A).
[37]*Amb.* 7 (1097B).
[38]On the unity of body and soul as indispensable to human identity, see Carolyn Walker Bynum, *The Resurrection of the Body in Western Christianity, 200–1336* (New York: Columbia University Press, 1995). Bynum does not discuss the writings of Maximus but she gives a very thorough account of the development of Christian thinking on soul and body.

aration from the soul "is not simply called body, but the body of a man, indeed the body of a certain man, even though it will decompose and be broken down into the elements of which it was composed. . . . Therefore the human being is composed of soul and body, for soul and body are indissolubly understood to be parts of the whole human species."[39] The issue is so crucial to his correction of Origenism that Maximus resumes a lengthy discussion of it in *Ambiguum* 42, where he describes the distinctive but connected origins of body and soul, and their synthesis in a single human species, and more importantly, the assumption by the New Adam of the first Adam's soul-body constitution.[40] In the incarnation, the Logos who created universal humanity fashioned his own manhood in a (prelapsarian) Adamic perfection; he himself modeled the perfect coexistence of intelligent soul and material body.

While much attention has rightly been paid to the anti-Origenist polemic operative in Maximus's long discourse in *Ambiguum* 7, the text's ultimate significance, like that of the *Ambigua* as a whole, must be measured in relation to his larger theological and spiritual enterprise. Seen this way, the correction of the Origenist myth is simply one component (an important one at that) in Maximus's integrative cosmic vision in which the economies of creation-deification, on the one hand, and (postlapsarian) intervention-redemption, on the other, merge as one dramatic plot whose "thickness" and internal connections can only truly be discerned from the standpoint of the mystery which *is* Jesus Christ,[41] the "mystery hidden throughout the ages" (Col 1:26)[42] that discloses the providence and judgment of God operative in the *logoi* of creation.

[39] *Amb.* 7 (PG 91:1101B).

[40] See *Amb.* 42 (PG 91:1316C–1317C, 1321B–1325B).

[41] See *Ad Thal.* 60 (CCSG 22:73, 5–10). "Christ" and the "mystery of Christ" are one and the same thing, in the sense that the whole universal mystery of salvation and deification is recapitulated deep within the individual "composite hypostasis" of the incarnate Logos.

[42] See *Amb.* 7 (PG 91:1097Bff).

Ambiguum 8 is largely an extended footnote to *Ambiguum* 7, revisiting the dilemma of how divine providence can be operative amid the weakness and suffering of corporeal existence, and with that the question of why human beings find themselves in such disparate bodily conditions. For Maximus, Gregory Nazianzen has already pointed to a solution by emphasizing the instability or chaos (τὸ ἄτακτον) latent in material, bodily existence. To be sure, the fall and the mortality and mutability that are its consequences have left created bodies weak and stunted. And like Gregory of Nyssa, Maximus is pressed to account for whether and how God foreknew the fall and shaped bodies accordingly when he co-created them with souls (a counter to the Origenist teaching that pre-incarnate souls fell into bodies suited to the degree of their sin). On the other hand, bodies, in their partnership with souls, have been created for ultimate deification. The mystery of *embodiment* is not constrained by a divine "adjustment" to the fall; rather, *teleologically* speaking, bodies are called into partnership with souls to attain to full communion with God. Historical, bodily existence is marked by inequalities and ambiguities, but these have become the very resources, as it were, out of which arises the new creature in Christ. Maximus sets in relief the deeply biblical theme of creation as a continuing act of divine resourcefulness: preserving, renewing, and transforming.

In *Ambiguum* 8, as he does consistently elsewhere, Maximus draws out the ascetical implications of his cosmic theology. The great frontier for rectifying the dilemma of bodily weakness and inequality is the healing of the human passions which betray the penchant toward "chaos" that constantly attends life in the flesh. Maximus highlights the divine pedagogy that oversees the errant impulses and affections of embodied human beings. We must either learn severely, by God's direct purgation and reorientation; or we must learn through our own present experiences to train ourselves against evil passions; or else, as Maximus further explains, we must look to imitate the example of the truly virtuous. In any event, exploiting Gregory Nazianzen's metaphor, humanity must resist

allowing the "flowing stream" of bodily (passible) existence to be
subverted by the undercurrent of chaos. Bodily life may conduct us
along in a way not completely in our control, but we are able to resist
in acts of mortification and humility that serve at once to stabilize
our own souls and to "equalize" the inequalities of life that are visible all around us.

One other important text setting forth the ethical exigencies of
Maximus's cosmic theology is *Ad Thalassium* 64, a short commentary on the book of Jonah, toward the end of which he describes the
three universal laws operative in the economy of salvation and deification: the natural law, the scriptural law, and the law of grace. This
is a familiar theme in Maximus, and has clear antecedents in Paul,
Origen, and Augustine. The three laws represent God's gracious and
benevolent (yet also punitive) plan for the world, with the natural law
and scriptural law subservient to the transcending *spiritual* law of the
grace of the incarnate Christ. As Hans Urs von Balthasar has pointed
out, however, the "synthesis" of the three laws is no simple collapsing
of the first two laws into the third, but a christological and soteriological interrelation in which each of the three plays its own irreducible role in the economy of human deification.[43] As Maximus
explains in *Ad Thalassium* 64, each law has its own proper discipline
(ἀγωγή) and its own place within the gospel of Jesus. The natural law
trains us in the basic solidarity and single-mindedness appropriate to
individual human beings who share a common nature; it is
enshrined in Jesus's Golden Rule (Mt 7:12; Lk 6:31). The scriptural law
leads to a higher discipline wherein human beings are motivated no
longer by the mere fear of divine punishment but by a deep-seated
embrace of the principle of mutual love. "For the law of nature,"
writes Maximus, "consists in natural reason assuming control of
the senses, while the scriptural law, or the fulfillment of the scriptural
law, consists in the natural reason acquiring a spiritual desire conducive to a relation of mutuality with others of the same human

[43]Von Balthasar, *Kosmische Liturgie*, pp. 288ff; see also Blowers, *Exegesis and Spiritual Pedagogy in Maximus the Confessor*, pp. 117–22.

nature."[44] The essence of the scriptural law is thus summarized in Jesus's dictum *Love your neighbor as yourself* (Lev 19:18; Mt 5:43; 19:19; 22:39; Mk 12:31). Finally, the spiritual law, or law of grace, leads humanity to the ultimate imitation of the love of Christ demonstrated in the incarnation, a love which raises us to the level of loving others even above ourselves, a sure sign of the radical grace of deification. It is enshrined in Jesus's teaching that *There is no greater love than this, that a man lay down his life for his friend* (Jn 15:13).

As Maximus further concludes, the three laws exhibit the principal ends to which human nature is called: the natural law grants us the fundamental enjoyment of *being* (τὸ εἶναι), the scriptural law the enjoyment of a higher *well-being* (τὸ εὖ εἶναι), the spiritual law the beatific grace of *eternal well-being* (τὸ ἀεὶ εὖ εἶναι).

The Adamic Dilemma: The Fall and the Origin of the Human Passions

If *Ambigua* 7 and 8 interpret human passibility (πάθος) within a broader cosmological and philosophical—albeit thoroughly christocentric—perspective,[45] other texts from *Ad Thalassium* explore the precise origins of this liability to passions and the role of the passions in the construction of a theological anthropology.

This complex set of questions had already exercised Maximus's predecessor Gregory of Nyssa, whose insights he carefully incorporates. No one in the Greek patristic tradition prior to Maximus had developed a more sophisticated response to Origenism and compelling explanation of the dynamics of the fall than the bishop of Nyssa. Gregory's contribution was to subsume the passions within a carefully nuanced doctrine of freedom, portraying human choice (beginning with Adam) as standing midway between the "two trees" of the garden, two competing motions, the proclivity toward blessed freedom in the Good and the proclivity toward those pleasures

[44] *Ad Thal.* 64 (CCSG 22:235, 768–772).
[45] See especially *Amb.* 7 (PG 91:1073Bff).

(experienced as "relative" goods) that lead to death.[46] Because Adam originally forfeited his quasi-angelic state of freedom, resulting in God's imposing bodily mortality and passibility (the "garments of skins," Gen 3:21) on the race, humanity has henceforth remained locked in an existential tug-of-war in which, it seems, the Good cannot be embraced without ascetically resisting an opposite tendency, even though the opposite is a metaphysical non-entity, an illusion "invented," as it were, by humankind.[47]

Maximus's debt to Gregory of Nyssa on this point is explicit in *Ad Thalassium* 1 on the origin of the passions. For both writers, the liability to passions epitomizes the ambiguity of embodied, historical existence, which has nevertheless become, through Jesus Christ, the frontier of the moral potentiality and spiritual "utility" (χρῆσις) of the passions. Maximus therefore carefully distinguishes between that passibility (πάθος, τὸ πάθον), or capacity for being moved by God toward a final end ("eternal well-being"),[48] which is *natural* to creatures, and the liability (τὸ πάθον, τὸ παθητός)[49] to deviant and diffusive movements of the "passions" (πάθη) like lust, pleasure, fear, and grief, that threaten to disintegrate the harmony of soul and body. The latter are accidents of experience, and yet in Maximus's urge to redeem rather than annihilate, even these passions, these "gentiles" of the soul as he calls them,[50] can, through transmutation, find a place in the economy of salvation and deification. Most basi-

[46]Gregory of Nyssa, *In Cant., Hom.* 12 (GNO 6:345, 11–346, 2). For a superb recent analysis of Nyssa's teaching on this theme, especially in his exegesis of Genesis and the Song of Songs, see Richard A. Norris, "Two Trees in the Midst of the Garden (Genesis 2:9b): Gregory of Nyssa and the Puzzle of Human Evil," in *In Dominico Eloquio— In Lordly Eloquence: Essays on Patristic Exegesis in Honor of Robert Louis Wilken*, ed. Paul M. Blowers, Angela Russell Christman, David G. Hunter, and Robin Darling Young (Grand Rapids: Eerdmans, 2001), pp. 218–41.

[47]Gregory of Nyssa, *De virginitate* 12 (GNO 8, pt. 1:298, 21–299, 12).

[48]Again see *Amb.* 7 (PG 91:1073Bff); also *Ad Thal.* 21 (CCSG 7:129, 50–52), where Maximus contrasts "natural passibility" (τὸ κατὰ φύσιν πάθος) and "unnatural passibility" (τὸ παρὰ φύσιν πάθος).

[49]See e.g. *Ad Thal.* 21 (CCSG 7:127, 14, 20, 27); ibid. 42 (CCSG 7:285, 18–28).

[50]*Ad Thal.* 51 (CCSG 7:403, 154–405, 189).

cally, one needs erotic desire (ἐπιθυμία), converted through love (ἀγάπη), to cling ardently to God, just as one needs the ire and indignation of the irascible faculty (θυμός) to fend off vice; in principle, a wide array of tractable passions could be reoriented in the service of the spiritual life.[51]

Ad Thalassium 21 and 61 provide some of Maximus's most extensive reflection on the legacy of Adam's fall and the history, as it were, of human passibility. Maximus muses even less than Gregory on the "angelic" life of Adam before the fall; he downplays it doubtless for fear that the "garments of skins" (Gen 3:21), like Origen's bodies, might still be interpreted only as secondarily and punitively imposed.[52] In fact God created Adam already with *the faculty of spiritual pleasure*, a sublime possibility. But the state of impassibility (ἀπάθεια), the perfect harmony of the passions with the mind, was more a potency than an actuality, since the original paradise in which Adam dwelled was *not yet* the state of deification projected as humanity's *telos*. Adam thereupon lapsed "at the instant he was created" (ἅμα τῷ γίνεσθαι),[53] squandering his faculty for spiritual pleasure and plunging his posterity into a tragic slavery to deviant passions. Parsing his definition of "original sin," the Confessor makes clear that we inherit not Adam's own sin itself (though humanity has certainly continued to imitate his disobedience); rather, we inherit that generic "sin" that is its consequence: passibil-

[51]On this theme in Maximus's anthropology, see Paul M. Blowers, "Gentiles of the Soul: Maximus the Confessor on the Substructure and Transformation of the Human Passions," *Journal of Early Christian Studies* 4 (1996): 57–85; and Robert L. Wilken, "Maximus the Confessor on the Affections in Historical Perspective," in *Asceticism*, ed. Vincent Wimbush and Richard Valantasis (New York: Oxford University Press, 1995), pp. 412–23. On the broader notion of how, according to the Greek Fathers, the passible "garments of skins" (Gen 3:21) are converted to good use in the scheme of salvation, see Nellas, *Deification in Christ*, pp. 43–91.

[52]On this point, see the fuller discussion of Thunberg, *Microcosm and Mediator*, pp. 144–54. For a full discussion of the dimensions of human corporeality in Maximus's thought, see Adam Cooper, "Holy Flesh, Wholly Deified: The Place of the Body in the Theological Vision of Maximus the Confessor" (Ph.D. dissertation, University of Durham, 2002).

[53]*Ad Thal.* 61 (CCSG 22:85, 8–16); *Amb.* 42 (PG 91:1320B).

ity, corruptibility, and mortality (*Ad Thal.* 21). Indeed, Maximus portrays this destiny both as an abiding dialectic of physical pleasure and pain (*Ad Thal.* 61) and as a subjugation to the law of sexual procreation (γέννησις) superadded to humanity's true origin (γένεσις), wherewith the powerful drive of sexual pleasure perpetuates the Adamic tragedy from generation to generation (*Ad Thal.* 21). In his own words, "The more human nature sought to preserve itself through sexual procreation, the more tightly it bound itself to the law of sin, reactivating the transgression connected with the liability to passions."[54]

In *Ad Thalassium* 21 and 42 Maximus also measures this legacy in the register of human volition. The ambiguity of embodied, historical existence reveals itself not only in the passions that waver between deviance and tractability, but in the stunted "gnomic" will (γνώμη) that accompanies humanity's "mixed" knowledge after the fall. Contrasted both with the "natural will" (θέλησις φυσική) created for communion with God, and with the "free choice" (προαίρεσις) that Adam enjoyed in an immutable state before the fall, the gnomic will has to deliberate in seeking the Good, and therein betrays its close association with the passions. Indeed, its vacillation goes hand in hand with the lust for pleasure and the fear of death that drive fallen humanity. Yet like the passions, Maximus, at least in his earlier writings, envisions the possibility of gnomic will, as a natural faculty, also being redeemed to good use in the moral and spiritual life of the Christian, as it functions precisely in our concrete human experience of grappling with vice and learning and growing in virtue.[55]

[54]*Ad Thal.* 21 (CCSG 7:127, 24–27).

[55]The incarnation, argues Maximus, has opened up an "inclinational (γνωμική) and volitional (προαιρητική) change and alteration" for humanity (*Comm. in Ps. 59*, CCSG 23:3, 8–12). The ascetic life itself is characterized by love's persuasion of γνώμη (*Ep.* 2, PG 91:396C). The gnomic will is to be transformed by the Holy Spirit (*Ad Thal.* 6, CCSG 7:71, 43–48), serves our spiritual progress (cf *Capita de caritate* 3.25, PG 90:1024B–C; ibid. 4.90, 1069C; *Opusc.* 4, PG 91:57A–B), and will in fact participate in

Jesus Christ and the Transformation of Human Passibility

The key to Maximus's teaching on the fall, human passibility, and the universality of sin, is his conviction that the incarnate Christ assumes the whole legacy of human fallenness while not wavering from the divine initiative toward the deification of creation. In *Ambiguum* 42, for example, he makes much of the fact that in the singular action of his incarnation, the Savior fused the "creaturely origin" (γένεσις) of humanity with a "birth" (γέννησις) subject to the procreative conditions of *fallen* humanity *yet without sin* (cf Heb 4:15). Only by perfectly merging these two things does he reveal himself truly as the New Adam.[56]

Rather than directly addressing the age-old question as to whether the incarnation would even have taken place had Adam not fallen, Maximus begins, as was noted earlier, with the mystery of the incarnation itself (Eph 1:3–23; Col 1:15–23, 26; 1 Cor 2:7; 15:28; Heb 4:15) as the lens through which to interpret the protology and the teleology of the universe.[57] A number of extraordinary passages in Maximus's corpus boldly display his christocentrism and his debt to the Pauline theology of the mystery of Christ. *Ambiguum 7* (sections 1096B–1097D) is undoubtedly central, but it is paralleled and amplified by *Ad Thalassium* 60, an uncontested *locus classicus* in the Confessor's writings. The scriptural text in question here concerns God's foreknowledge of Christ as the "pure and spotless lamb" (1 Pet 1:20), the figure of whom appears prominently in Byzantine iconography.[58] Maximus eloquently eulogizes Jesus Christ, the perfect hypostatic union of divine and human natures, as already constituting in

---

deification, as indicated by Maximus's notion of a "willing surrender," or literally "gnomic emigration" (ἐκχώρησις γνωμικὴ) into God (*Amb.* 7, PG 91:1076B–C).

[56]*Amb.* 42 (PG 91:1316C–1317B).

[57]See Larchet's extensive discussion in *La divinisation de l'homme selon saint Maxime le Confesseur*, pp. 221–382. See also David Yeago, "Jesus of Nazareth and Cosmic Redemption," pp. 163–93.

[58]A splendid example is the Lamb enshrined in the sanctuary dome of the Church of San Vitale in Ravenna, completed just a few decades before Maximus was born.

himself the fullness of the "Christic mystery" (τὸ κατὰ Χριστὸν μυστήριον), the comprehensive outworking of the divine plan (Eph 1:10–11) for the redemption and deification of the world which God premeditated before the ages. Equally importantly, however, Maximus locates the incarnation within a trinitarian matrix. The Three Persons foreknew the incarnation and shared mutually in its realization: the Father approving it, the Son properly carrying it out, the Spirit cooperating in it. This, for Maximus, is the gracious economy which encloses the whole of human history and makes possible both our rational knowledge of God and, more sublimely, our *experiential* participation in the mystery of deification.

If in *Ad Thalassium* 60 Maximus contemplates the mystery of Christ as divinely foreknown and predetermined before all the ages (1 Pet 1:20; Col 1:26; 1 Cor 2:7), in *Ad Thalassium* 22 he enhances the properly *eschatological* dimension of the mystery. Christ is indeed the mystery hidden before the ages, but he is also the mystery at the end of the ages (1 Cor 10:11). Maximus waxes eloquent on the different possible senses of "the ages" in the Apostle's usage, but clearly in his interpretation of Paul more is at stake than a mere sequence of ages of time. Christ comprehends both the "ages" of divine incarnation ("the mystery of God's embodiment") and the "ages" of creaturely deification. The former have been consummated in the coming of Jesus, but so too the latter have already commenced, though there remains that definitive "end" (τέλος) when natural creatures, receiving in full the grace of the incarnation, will undergo an utter transformation, rendered thoroughly passive to divine grace: the ultimate "passion" of deification.[59]

Not surprisingly, given the shared concern of Maximus and Thalassius to situate the ascetic life within the larger mystery of deification, a number of the *Quaestiones ad Thalassium* address the issue

---

[59]Maximus variously describes deification as a sublime "experience" (πεῖρα) (*Ad Thal.* 6, CCSG 7:69, 23–24; 71, 46–48); a "pleasurable suffering" (πεῖσις) (*Amb.* 7, PG 91:1088C–D); and a "supernatural passion" (ὑπὲρ φύσιν τὸ πάθος) (*Ad Thal.* 22 (CCSG 7:139, 66–141, 98). According to *Ad Thal.* 59 (CCSG 22:55, 156–157), it is also the most ineffable "pleasure" (ἡδονή) and "enjoyment" (χαρά).

of how precisely the incarnation of God in Jesus Christ inaugurated
a transformation at the level of human passibility, a transformation
that turned the very stigma of our fallen nature into a resource for
ultimate personal communion with God. Generally speaking,
within these texts Maximus intends to show how Christ took on
himself *natural* human passibility, even the liability to deviant passions, but not the postlapsarian peccability which for Adam's posterity has stymied the good use of the possible faculties. In so doing
Christ not only resolves the legacy of the fall but pioneers a whole
new modality (τρόπος) for human passion consistent with the soul's
natural—and perpetually graced—desire for God.

In *Ad Thalassium* 21, for example, the text of Colossians 2:15 has
puzzled Thalassius. The Greek is quite graphic in describing Christ
as "putting off" or literally "divesting himself of" (ἀπεκδυσάμενος)
the wicked powers and principalities in his incarnation. Such must
imply that he "put them on" (ἐνδυσάμενος) in the first place, which
seems entirely inconsistent with presuppositions about Christ's
immaculate conception and birth. Maximus exploits this exegetical
aporion and so revisits an ancient christological dilemma. Here, as in
Ambiguum 42, he argues that Christ entered the world consistent
with Adam's creaturely origin (γένεσις) and created dignity, but what
is more, for our sake, he subjected himself to the postlapsarian procreative process of human birth (γέννησις) in order that he might
take on the liability to deviant passions—*yet without sin* (Heb 4:15).[60]
We know of this liability because Christ was inevitably tempted, from
the desert to the Passion, and *used* this testing precisely in order to
dupe the opportunistic "powers and principalities" enslaving our
passions and so heal our human passibility from within.

Maximus takes the same tack in *Ad Thalassium* 42, where he
carefully elucidates Paul's bold assertion that Christ "became sin" on

---

[60]The pivotal text of Heb 4:15 provides the axis for the study of Maximus's Christology by Guido Bausenhart, *In Allem uns gleich ausser der Sunde: Studien zum Beitrag
Maximos' des Bekenners zur altchristlichen Christologie*, Tübinger Studien zur Theologie und Philosophie 5 (Mainz: Matthias Grünewald, 1995).

our behalf (1 Cor 5:21). Demonstrating his exegetical sophistication, Maximus identifies the equivocation of the term "sin" in Scripture and concludes that Christ "became" not the causal, culpable "sin" committed by Adam and all his posterity who imitate him, but the *consequential* "sin that I caused" (ἡ δι᾽ ἐμὲ ἁμαρτία), namely, the passibility, corruptibility, and mortality that have been introduced into human nature. Here, as in *Ad Thalassium* 21, the Confessor explores in depth the interior mystery of Christ as the New Adam, the bearer and pioneer of eschatological humanity. At this juncture, long before the Monothelite controversy, Maximus was far more concerned with the dilemma, born of the controversy over Origenism, of how Christ resolves the mutability (τροπή) of human volition and, concomitantly, the vulnerability or deviance of the human passions. Without hesitation, then, he ascribes to Christ an immutable power of free choice (προαίρεσις) as the means by which the Savior reoriented not only human free choice but the more existentially fragile gnomic will. Interestingly, in his *Commentary on the Lord's Prayer* (written probably just a few years before the *Ad Thalassium*) he had openly ascribed to Christ himself the possession of a gnomic will (γνώμη) perfectly fixed on the Good, though in *Ad Thalassium* 21 and 42 he already appears to shy away from such an attribution.[61] Later on, correcting himself even more precisely in the heat of the Monothelite crisis, he would deny both prohairetic and gnomic will in Christ in affirming the pure integrity of Christ's natural human will (θέλημα, θέλησις).[62] The change may already be hinted at in *Ad Thalassium* 61, when Maximus, carefully choosing his terms, states that while humanity had fallen into sin through gnomic will (κατὰ γνώμην), "[Christ] exhibited the equity of his justice in the magnitude of his condescension, when he *willingly* (κατὰ θέλησιν) submitted to the condemnation imposed on our passibility and turned that very passibility into an instrument for

----

[61]See the translation and notes for *Ad Thalassium* 21 and 42 below.
[62]Cf *Opusc.* 3 (PG 91:56A–D); *Opusc.* 16 (192B–C); *Disputatio cum Pyrrho* (PG 91:308C–309A, 311A–313C).

eradicating sin and the death which is its consequence—or in other words, for eradicating pleasure and the pain which is its consequence."[63]

Christ's human freedom and possible gnomic will have been a continuing debating-point in contemporary interpretations of Maximus's Christology, and for good reason. For how can the individuated gnomic wills of the masses of fallen human beings be redeemed if Christ himself has not assumed *gnōmē*? Maximus never seems to have resolved this issue directly. Once he had categorically denied gnomic will in Christ for fear of attributing vacillation to the Savior, we can only assume that he believed that the stabilization of *our* gnomic wills went hand in hand with the reorientation of the whole possible self accomplished through the perfect human will (θέλησις) of Christ operative in the hypostatic union.[64]

Opusculum 6, composed (ca. 641) during the transition into christological controversy that dominated the Confessor's later career, and giving us a glimpse of Maximus's sometimes tenacious theological logic, reveals the maturing of his reflection on this set of questions. *Ad Thalassium* 21 had broached the temptation or testing of Christ in the full sweep of his earthly ministry. Here in *Opusculum* 6, a text that François-Marie Léthel credits as the true breakthrough in Maximus's criticism of Monothelite Christology,[65] the scene shifts squarely to the intense drama of Gethsemane, when Jesus of Nazareth, in the particularity of a single historical moment, hands his human will (θέλησις) over to the will of the Father, thereby demonstrating the perfect concert of divine and human

[63] *Ad Thal.* 61 (CCSG 22:89, 85–90).

[64] For a recent reflection on these issues in Maximus, see Paul M. Blowers, "The Passion of Jesus Christ in Maximus the Confessor: A Reconsideration," *Studia Patristica* 37, ed. M. F. Wiles and E. J. Yarnold (Leuven: Peeters Press, 2001), especially pp. 366–71.

[65] François-Marie Léthel, *Théologie de l'agonie du Christ: la liberté humaine du Fils de Dieu et son importance sotériologique mises en lumière par saint Maxime le Confesseur*, Théologie historique 52 (Paris: Beauchesne, 1979), pp. 86ff, 103; also Léthel's Introduction to Marie-Hélène Congourdeau, ed. and trans., *Maxime le Confesseur: L'agonie du Christ*, Les pères dans la foi (Paris: Migne, 1996), pp. 7–20.

wills, free of all opposition or resistance, which makes possible the complete transformation of human passibility and mutability. In the later *Opuscula* 7 (ca. 642) and 3 (ca. 645–646), Maximus would expand at greater length on this magnificent interplay of wills in Gethsemane as a dramatic epitome of the incarnational economy as a whole.[66]

New Birth and the Christian's Progress in Virtue

Drawing from the spiritual treasury of the Bible, from the wisdom of the Fathers (especially the Cappadocians and Cyril of Alexandria), from the sages of his own Byzantine monastic tradition (figures as prolific as Evagrius in the fourth century and Sophronius in his own), from inspired mystical theologians like Pseudo-Dionysius the Areopagite, and from the breadth and depth of his own experience and theological ingenuity Maximus the Confessor generated his own synthetic vision of the spiritual life of the Christian as a micro-drama of the larger macro-drama of salvation history. Accordingly, all Christians are called to an "ascetic" life broadly understood, insofar as every believer must aspire, through disciplined practice (πρᾶξις) and contemplation (θεωρία), exercising every level of the life of the soul and the body, to participate in the transfiguration of the cosmos—indeed, to be a miniature demonstration of its realization—and thereby to share actively in Christ's mediation of the new creation.[67]

---

[66]Cf *Opusc.* 7 (PG 91:69B–89B); *Opusc.* 3 (45B–56D). Eng. trans. of these texts in Louth, *Maximus the Confessor*, pp. 180–98.

[67]Fortunately many of his major spiritual writings have already appeared in published English translations, and extensive studies of his spiritual doctrine have accompanied them. See especially Berthold, ed. and trans., *Maximus Confessor: Selected Writings*; also Polycarp Sherwood, ed. and trans., *St. Maximus the Confessor: The Ascetic Life and Four Centuries on Charity*, Ancient Christian Writers 21 (Westminster, Md.: Newman Press, 1957); also the substantial studies of Walther Völker, *Maximus Confessor als Meister des geistlichen Lebens* (Wiesbaden: Franz Steiner, 1965); Thunberg, *Microcosm and Mediator*, pp. 231–436; and Larchet, *La divinisation de l'homme*, especially chs. 8–12, pp. 399–676.

Given Maximus's integrative perspective, the pointing of his whole theological project toward the mystery of Jesus Christ, and the "deep structure" of his spirituality, no text in his corpus is irrelevant to his theology of the Christian life. The texts in this volume, however, most directly address his teaching on the conversion of human passibility as instrumental in the progress toward divinization. The consistent theme is Christ's vindication of the divine plan for creaturely deification and his pioneering of a new mode (τρόπος) for the whole of human nature, including the passible self and its faculties, which brings the Creator's plan to full fruition.

Baptism for Maximus is the new birth by the Spirit that roots the believer in this ongoing transformative process, this new existential *mode.* According to *Ambiguum* 42, baptism takes its place among the "three births" to which humanity is subject and which the Savior himself has honored: first, our original *coming-into-being* (γένεσις) as creatures made in the image of God; second, our *baptismal* birth, which confers the grace of "well-being"(τὸ εὖ εἶναι); and third, the ultimate birth of *resurrection,* whereby we attain to the grace of "eternal well-being" (τὸ ἀεὶ εὖ εἶναι).[68] Within this scheme, the incarnate Lord's own baptism—and now ours—secures for Adam's fallen posterity the spiritual birth and vocation that Adam himself had lost, a birth that shatters the bond of carnal birth and assures adoption in the Spirit, simultaneously restoring God's intended plan (λόγος) for Adam and his race.[69]

> For the Savior the sequence was, first of all, incarnation and bodily birth for my sake; and so thereupon the birth in the Spirit through baptism, originally spurned by Adam, for the sake of my salvation and restoration by grace, or, to describe it even more vividly, my remaking (ἀνάπλασις). God, as it were, connected for me the principle of my being and the principle of my well-being, bridging the separation and

[68]*Amb.* 42 (PG 91:1316A–1325C).
[69]*Amb.* 42 (PG 91:1348A–D); also Larchet, *La divinisation de l'homme,* pp. 237–8.

distance between them that I had caused, and thereby wisely drew them together in the principle of eternal being.[70]

Ad Thalassium 6 takes us further into the baptismal *vocation* as such. Here Thalassius recalls for Maximus the long-standing dilemma of postbaptismal sin. Given St John's exalted language of the one baptized with water and Spirit as truly "born of God," how is it even possible for the baptized believer to sin (Jn 3:5–6; 1 Jn 3:9)? Such a question had come up much earlier in Byzantine monastic tradition, particularly during the Messalian controversy, in which certain radical ascetics had questioned the efficacy of baptism to eradicate sin and secure the Christian in a state of impassibility.[71] Maximus's fifth-century predecessor Mark the Hermit, countering this Messalian anti-sacramentalism, wrote that "Christ, being perfect God, bestows on the baptized the grace of the Spirit. We add nothing to that grace; it is revealed to and manifested in us in proportion to our performance of the commandments, and provides us the added assistance of faith *until we all attain to perfect manhood, to the measure of the stature of the fullness of Christ* (Eph 4:10)."[72] In effect, baptism plants the seed of a grace that will continue to unfold itself in the penitent and fruit-bearing life of the believer. Maximus's response to Thalassius echoes the wisdom of this earlier tradition and brings to it his own fresh insights. Baptism, he indicates, actually entails two dimensions, two births in one. On the one hand it implants, through the believer's faith, the fully *potential* grace of adoption in the Spirit; on the other hand, it begins the *actualization* of that grace which must grow and continue through the believer's active assimilation to God. The latter, he observes, involves the conversion of free choice (προαίρεσις) and of the gnomic will

[70]*Amb.* 42 (PG 91:1348D).
[71]See Mark the Hermit, *De baptismo, quaest.* 1 (PG 65:985A); ibid. 4 (992D, 993A–B); also Kallistos Ware, "The Sacrament of Baptism and the Ascetic Life in the Teaching of Mark the Monk," *Studia Patristica* 10, Texte und Untersuchungen 107 (Berlin: Akademie-Verlag, 1970), pp. 441–52.
[72]Mark the Hermit, *De baptismo, resp.* 5 (PG 65:1008C).

(γνώμη) as well as the acquisition of a knowledge based on and enriched by our spiritual experience (πεῖρα). Clearly for Maximus, the baptismal vocation reveals a synergy of the Holy Spirit and the will of the graced Christian, yet he strongly emphasizes the burden on the believer to discipline the will, to stabilize personal inclination, since the Spirit does not compel an unwilling *gnōmē* nor baptism nullify its freedom. In his own words: "Even if we have the Spirit of adoption, who is himself the Seed for enduing those begotten (through baptism) with the likeness of the Sower, but do not present him with a will (γνώμη) cleansed of any inclination or disposition to something else, we therefore, even after being born of water and Spirit (Jn 3:5), willingly sin."[73]

In view of this vulnerability, the life to which the baptized Christian is called is a constant *ascesis,* a steadying of the mutable will and affections, a perpetual "retraining" as it were. Gregory of Nyssa famously dealt with this mutability (τροπή)—understood pejoratively as "deviance," or by the Origenists as the liability to "stall out" in the good through spiritual "surfeit" (κόρος)—by imagining the soul engaged in a *perpetual progress or striving* (ἐπέκτασις) to embrace its ultimate desirable, God.[74] Maximus appropriates Nyssa's concept, but not without revision.[75] Cautious that such perpetual change-for-the-better would simply amount to the soul's endless overcoming of an inherent capacity to stray from its true destiny or even to stall because of satiety, Maximus applies his distinction between a creature's mutable "mode of existence" (τρόπος ὑπάρξεως) and its ontologically prior "natural principle" (λόγος φύσεως), which comprehends and stabilizes its existential movements. Nevertheless, Maximus fundamentally concurs with

[73]*Ad Thal.* 6 (CCSG 7:71, 38–43).

[74]For a collection of texts evoking this theme in Gregory, see Herbert Musurillo, ed., *From Glory to Glory: Texts from Gregory of Nyssa's Mystical Writings* (reprint ed., Crestwood, N.Y.: St Vladimir's Seminary Press, 1979), § 16, 21, 43, 46, 50, 51, 53, 75, 155.

[75]For a detailed study of this appropriation, see Paul M. Blowers, "Maximus the Confessor, Gregory of Nyssa, and the Concept of 'Perpetual Progress,'" *Vigiliae Christianae* 46 (1992): 151–71.

Gregory that, because God is utterly infinite, and because the most natural human drive is an appetitive longing for the Divine, no creature can truly exhaust its progress (or be "sated") in communion with God.[76] Even in the afterlife, deification is an "ever-moving repose" (στάσις ἀεικίνητος) in God.[77]

The Nyssene image of the spiritual life as a perpetual striving toward the Good, an advancement "from glory to glory" (2 Cor 3:18), appears frequently in Maximus's early spiritual writings,[78] and is epitomized in *Ad Thalassium* 17, a text clearly influenced by Gregory's great treatise *The Life of Moses*. If he repudiates the Origenist idea that souls can potentially stall in a state of spiritual satiety, Maximus nonetheless acknowledges that the Christian ascetic can experience a "peaking out" perilously associated with the vice of vainglory.[79] The subject of *Ad Thalassium* 17 is an otherwise obscure narrative from Moses's career. God commissioned Moses to travel to Egypt, and en route he was stopped by an angel who indicted him for not having circumcised his son (Ex 4:19–26). Moses appears superficially innocent, having not been forewarned of the need to circumcise the boy. On the moral and spiritual level, however, this is a story of the divine commissioning of the soul to enter the "Egypt" of the heart and liberate godly thoughts. Moses symbolizes every ascetic mind (νοῦς) who, summoned to pursue the way of virtue but distracted by illusions and passions, fails to circumcise thoughts spiritually, thus inciting the word of God to enter like an angel and smite the conscience. For "the road of the virtues . . . in no way admits of any stalling on the part of those who walk in it . . . and the

[76]See *Amb.* 7 (PG 91:1069B, 1089B). See also Sherwood, *The Earlier Ambigua*, pp. 181–204.

[77]*Amb.* 67 (PG 91:1401A); *Ad Thal.* 59 (CCSG 22:53, 131); ibid. 65 (CCSG 22:285, 545–546); or the converse paradox of an everlasting "stationary identical movement" (στάσιμος ταυτοκινησία) (*Ad Thal.* 65, CCSG 22:285, 546).

[78]Cf *Capita theologica et oikonomica* ("Chapters on Knowledge") 1.35 (PG 90:1096C–1097A); ibid. 2.18 (1133A–B); ibid. 2.77 (1161A–B); *Capita de caritate* ("Chapters on Love") 3.46 (PG 90:1029C); *Mystagogia* 5 (PG 91:676C–677A).

[79]See von Balthasar, *Kosmische Liturgie*, p. 413.

immobility of virtue is the beginning of vice."[80] Citing Gregory of Nyssa's own cherished scriptural text, Paul's image of the runner straining to reach the victory line and striving toward *the goal of the upward call* in Christ (Phil 3:13–14), Maximus encourages all Christians to stay the course toward God, aided by a new kind of "angels," the principles (λόγοι) and modes (τρόποι) of the virtues.

For Maximus the Confessor, the Christian's growth in the grace of the Spirit is at once a progress of disciplined reasoning and will, but also a transformation at the level of appetite and of the soul's deep-seated desires. Deification in this perspective entails the ultimate alignment of the whole array of human affections with the soul's natural desire for God. It is, moreover, the final victory of love, the cosmic virtue that both reorients the passions and disposes the Christian in a perfect relation with God, with neighbor, and indeed with all creation.[81] As Maximus writes in an early letter to John the Cubicularius, dating around 626,

> Love gives faith the reality of what it believes and hope the presence of what it hopes for, and the enjoyment of what is present (cf 1 Cor 13:13; Heb 11:1). Love alone, properly speaking, proves that the human person is in the image of the Creator, by making his self-determination submit to reason, not bending reason under it, and persuading the inclination (γνώμη) to follow nature and not in any way to be at variance with the *logos* of nature. In this way we are all, as it were, one nature, so that we are able to have one inclination and one will (μία γνώμη καὶ θέλημα) with God and with one another, not having any discord with God or one another, whenever by the law of grace, through which by our inclination the law of nature is renewed, we choose what is ultimate.[82]

[80]*Ad Thal.* 17 (CCSG 7:113, 34–38).

[81]In addition to his trenchant *Chapters on Love*, see Maximus's encomium on the cosmic virtue of ἀγάπη in *Epistle* 2 (PG 91:392D–408B).

[82]*Ep.* 2 (PG 91:396C–D), trans. Louth, *Maximus the Confessor*, pp. 86–7.

On the Beginning and End of Rational Creatures

(PG 91:1068D–1101C)

[1068D] Gregory Nazianzen: "What does Wisdom have in mind for me? And what is this great mystery? Is it God's intention that we who are a portion of God and have slipped down from above should out of self-importance be so haughty and puffed up as to despise our Creator? Hardly! Rather we should always look to him in our struggle against the weakness of the body. Its very limitations are a form of training for those in our condition."[1]

I

[1069A] It seems that some who read these words are unable to find their true meaning even though they have expended great effort. They have pursued a facile solution and borrowed too much from Greek teachings. According to their opinion there once existed a single entity (ἑνάς) of rational beings. We were all connatural with God and had our *dwelling place* (Jn 14:2) and foundation in God. Then came movement from God and from this they make it out that, as rational beings were dispersed in various ways, God envisaged the

---

[1]Gregory Nazianzen, *Oration* 14.7 (*On Love for the Poor*) (PG 35:865C).

creation of this corporeal world to unite them with bodies as punishment for their former transgressions.[2] Those who hold these
things think that our teacher had intimated them in the words cited
above.[3]

[1069B] But they do not realize how untenable their views and
how improbable their conjectures, as a more reasonable argument
will surely demonstrate. For if the divine is unmoved, since it fills all
things, and everything that was brought from non-being to being is
moved (because it tends toward some end), then nothing that moves
is yet at rest. For movement driven by desire has not yet come to rest
in that which is ultimately desirable. Unless that which is ultimately
desirable is possessed, nothing else is of such a nature as to bring to
rest what is being driven by desire. Therefore if something moves it
has not come to rest, for it has not yet attained the ultimately desirable. Those who are tending toward that which is ultimately desirable
have not yet reached the end, since they have not yet come to rest.

[1069C] But if it is the case, as some hold, that rational beings had
in fact reached this end, and afterward were moved from their secure
abode in what is ultimately desirable, with the result that they were
scattered, we must ask in no uncertain words: what proof do they
have? For if this is so, it must be assumed that under similar circumstances rational beings will necessarily undergo such changes indefinitely. If God can be abandoned once for the sake of experiencing

[2]See Origen, De principiis 2.1.1: "Now since the world is so very varied and comprises so great a diversity of rational beings, what else can be the cause of this diversity than the different ways in which those who flowed away from the original unity
(ἑνάς) fell." Text from Justinian, Ep. ad Menan (Iustiniani Edictum Contra Originem)
in E. Schwartz, ed., Acta conciliorum oecumenicorum 3:211 (= G. D. Mansi, ed., Sacrorum conciliorum nova et amplissima collectio 9:529).

[3]Barsanuphius, a monk from Gaza in the early sixth century, said that some who
believed in the pre-existence of souls appealed to the writings of Gregory the Theologian (Ep. 604). See also Cyril of Scythopolis: the Origenists "affirm that the doctrines of pre-existence and restoration are indifferent and without danger, citing the
words of Saint Gregory" (Life of Cyriacus 11). Gregory Nazianzen, according to a sixth-
century life, was "the only one to be called 'the theologian' after the evangelist John"
(Gregory the Presbyter, Life of Gregory, PG 35:288C). Gregory's authority was second
only to that of the Holy Scriptures.

something different, there is nothing to prevent this from happening again and again. If reasonable beings are thus to be carried about and have no place to rest and cannot hope to have any abiding steadfastness in the good,[4] what could be greater reason to despair?[5]

On the other hand, if our opponents should say that intellects could have adhered to the divine goodness, but did not, because they wanted to experience something different, then the beautiful would of necessity be loved not for itself, but because of what had been learned of it from its opposite. That would mean the beautiful is loved for some other reason than that it is itself lovable by nature. What is not good and lovable in itself, and does not draw all movement toward it simply because it is good and lovable, cannot properly be the beautiful. [1069D] Such beauty would be incapable of satisfying the desire of those who find delight in it. In fact those who hold this view would have to be grateful to evil, because it taught them what is right and how to hold firmly to the beautiful. [1072A] If our opponents are consistent, they would say that evil brought things into being and is more useful than nature itself, because in their view evil teaches what is fitting and allows one to attain the most precious possession, I mean love, by which all things made by God are brought back to abide in God forever.

Further, of the things made by God, whether intellectual or sensible, coming into being precedes movement.[6] It is impossible to have movement before something has come into being. If the movement of things that have come into being is of intellectual things, it is intellectual movement, and if it is of sensible things, it is sensible movement. [1072B] As is apparent to those who have examined

---

[4]The phrase "steadfastness in the good" occurs in Gregory of Nyssa's *Life of Moses* 199 (GNO 7, pt. 1: 102, 19–21).

[5]Augustine makes a similar point. Our present concern, he writes, "is to combat the theory of cycles." . . . (*Civ. Dei* 12.20).

[6]Elsewhere Maximus writes: "Before we think of any natural movement of things, we must think of their becoming; but movement must naturally be presupposed as prior to all rest. . . . Therefore it is impossible for becoming and rest to come into existence at the same time, since they are naturally separated from each other through the middle term of movement" (*Amb.* 15, PG 91:1217D).

these things carefully, no creature is by nature unmoved, not even those that are inanimate and perceptible by the senses. All movement is either linear, circular or spiral, that is it is either simple [linear] or complex [circular or spiral].[7] If, then, coming into being is understood to precede movement, movement is subsequent to coming into being.[8]

The movement that is tending toward its proper end is called a natural power, or passion, or movement passing from one thing to another and having impassibility as its end. It is also called an irrepressible activity that has as its end perfect fulfillment.[9] But nothing that comes into being is its own end, since it is not self-caused. [1072C] For if it were, it would be unbegotten, without beginning and unmoved, since it has nothing toward which it can be moved in any way. For what is self-caused transcends what has come into being, because it exists for the sake of nothing. Hence the definition is correct even though it was spoken by an outsider: "The end is that for the sake of which all things exist, it, however, is for the sake of nothing."[10]

[7]Pseudo-Dionysius the Areopagite: "The divine intelligences are said to move as follows. First they move in a circle while they are at one with those illuminations which, without beginning and without end, emerge from the Good and the Beautiful. Then they move in a straight line when, out of Providence, they come to offer unerring guidance to all those below them. Finally, they move in a spiral, for when while they are providing for those beneath them they continue to remain what they are and they turn unceasingly around the Beautiful and the Good from which all identity comes" (*Divine Names* 4.8, PG 3:704D–705A; trans. Colm Luibheid, *Pseudo-Dionysius: The Complete Works*, CWS [Mahwah, N.J.: Paulist Press, 1987], p. 78).

[8]For the Origenists the order of things coming into being was the following: stability, motion, becoming (γένεσις); for Maximus: becoming, motion, stability. "It cannot be squared with the truth to propose that becoming is prior to stability, since stability is of its nature without motion; but it is equally impossible to posit stability as the consequence of a motionless becoming, or to equate stability and becoming. For stability is not a potential condition of becoming. . . . but is rather the end-stage of the realization of potency in the development of created things. To put it briefly, stability is a relative concept, which is not related to becoming but to movement, of which it is the contradictory" (*Amb.* 15, PG 91:1220C–D).

[9]As Sherwood observes: "The Maximian refutation [of the Origenist position] here starts from the idea of motion as essentially directed to an end" (*The Earlier Ambigua*, p. 98).

[10]The definition is Aristotelian, but as Sherwood observes, it is not a direct

Nothing that came into being is perfect in itself and complete. If complete it would have the power of action, but because it has its being from what is not, it does not have power of action. That which is perfect in itself is uncaused. Nor is anything that has come into being free of passions. Only what is unique, infinite and uncircumscribed is free of passions. The impassible is not of a nature to suffer at all, whether by loving another or by being moved by desire toward something else. No created thing then is at rest until it has attained the first and only cause (from which what exists was brought into being) or has possessed the ultimately desirable. [1072D] However, in the view of some, it was the breakup of the primordial unity that brought about the origin of bodies.

The saints Moses and David and Paul as well as Christ the Lord bear witness to the true understanding of these things.[11] Speaking of the first parents, Moses wrote. *You shall not eat of the tree of life* (Gen 2:9, 17). And elsewhere he said: *For you have not as yet come to the rest*[12] *and the inheritance which the Lord your God gives you* (Deut 12:9). [1073A] And David: *Crying out I will be satisfied when your glory appears* (Ps 16:15). And: *My soul thirsts for the strong and living God* (Ps 42:2).

And St Paul writes: *That if possible I may attain the resurrection from the dead. Not that I have already obtained this or am already perfect, but I press on to make it my own, because Christ Jesus has made me his own* (Phil 3:11). And to the Hebrews[13] he writes: *For whoever*

citation. For similar statements in Aristotle's works see *Metaphysics* 999B8f and *De motu animalium* 700B15. Maximus's language approximates that of Alexander of Aphrodisiac in *Metaphysics* B2 (*Commentaria in Aristotolem Graeca* 1:181, 37ff). But Sherwood thinks Maximus may be quoting an aphorism of Evagrius preserved in Syriac. "The milieu of the definition, then, is beyond doubt. It is then the more piquant to know that the outsider cited is none other than Evagrius" (*The Earlier Ambigua*, p. 100). Nonetheless, it seems more likely to me that "outsider" refers to Aristotle.

[11]The theme of the biblical texts cited by Maximus in this section is that things have not come to fulfillment.

[12]Note that the term "rest" is biblical. See also Heb 4:10 cited at 1073A.

[13]In the early church Paul was considered the author of the Epistle to the Hebrews.

enters into God's rest also ceases from his labors as God did from his
(Heb 4:10). And again in the same epistle he affirms that no one
received what was promised (Heb 11:39).

Also Christ says: *Come to me all you who labor and are heavy
laden and I will give you rest* (Matt 11:28). [1073B] Therefore no creature has ever ceased using the inherent power that directs it towards
its end, nor has it ceased the natural activity that impels it towards
its end, nor harvested what it had anticipated. I am referring of
course to being impassible and unmoved. For it belongs to God
alone to be the end and the completion and the impassible. God is
unmoved and complete and impassible. It belongs to creatures to be
moved toward that end which is without beginning, and to come to
rest in the perfect end that is without end, and to experience[14] that
which is without definition, but not to *be* such or to *become* such in
essence. For whatever comes into being and is created is certainly not
absolute.

It is important to understand correctly what is meant by passibility (πάθος). For the passibility spoken of in this connection does
not refer to change or corruption of one's power; passibility here
indicates that which exists by nature in beings. For everything that
comes into existence is subject to movement, since it is not self-
moved or self-powered. [1073C] If then rational beings come into
being, surely they are also moved, since they move from a natural
beginning in "being" toward a voluntary end in "well-being." For the
end of the movement of those who are moved is "eternal well-being"
itself, just as its beginning is being itself which is God who is the giver
of being as well as of well-being.[15] For God is the beginning and the

[14]The term is παθεῖν: "suffer," "be acted upon," "undergo."

[15]On being and well-being: The "*logos* of being . . . denotes the created existence
of a thing as founded in God's will that it should be, it is the principle of its coming
to be and implies a participation in God as being." The "*logos* of well-being . . .
expresses participation in God as good and is the principle of motion in each being,
i.e. logos as regulating moral action and will" (Lars Thunberg, *Microcosm and Mediator*, p. 74). "Well-being" is identified with acquiring the "likeness of God." There is a
third mode, "eternal well-being" (τὸ ἀεὶ εὖ εἶναι) (PG 91:1392B). Cf *Chapters on Love*

end. From him come both our moving in whatever way from a beginning and our moving in a certain way toward him as an end.

If the intellectual being is moved intellectually in a way appropriate to itself, it certainly perceives. If it perceives, it certainly loves what it perceives. If it loves, it certainly experiences ecstasy (ἔκστα-σις) over what is loved.[16] If it experiences ecstasy, it presses on eagerly, and if it presses on eagerly it intensifies its motion; [1073D] if its motion is intensified, it does not come to rest until it is embraced wholly by the object of its desire. It no longer wants anything from itself, for it knows itself to be wholly embraced, and intentionally and by choice it wholly receives the lifegiving delimitation. When it is wholly embraced it no longer wishes to be embraced at all by itself but is suffused by that which embraces it. [1076A] In the same way air is illuminated by light and iron is wholly inflamed by fire, as is the case with other things of this sort.

From such speculation we are able to understand that participation in a goodness that is yet to come not one that existed once and was corrupted. The saints will participate in it, though only through a likeness,[17] since what is hoped for is beyond all things, beyond vision and hearing and understanding, as is clear from the Scriptures (cf 1 Cor 2:9–11).

What is being referred to is that subjection about which the divine apostle spoke, when the Son subjects to the Father those who freely accept subjection (1 Cor 15:28). This subjection will be voluntary, and through it the last enemy, death, will be destroyed. [1076B]

3.24–25; also *Chapters on Theology and Economy* 1:56: "The sixth day reveals the principle of being of things, the seventh indicates the manner of the well-being of things, the eighth communicates the ineffable mystery of the eternal well-being of things" (PG 90:1104C). See also *Amb.* 42 (PG 91:1325B–C, translated below, pp. 88–9). Other references in Sherwood, *The Earlier Ambigua*, p. 67, n. 27; and von Balthasar, *Kosmische Liturgie*, pp. 622–3.

[16]On Maximus's understanding of "ecstasy" and sublime passivity, see Sherwood, *The Earlier Ambigua*, pp. 124–54; and Larchet, *La divinisation de l'homme*, pp. 533–45.

[17]Cf Ezek. 1:26 where Ezekiel says that in his vision he saw "the likeness as it were of a human being."

That which is in our power, our free will, through which the power
of corruption entered into us, will surrender voluntarily to God and
will have mastery of itself because it had been taught to refrain from
willing anything other than what God wills. As our Savior himself
said, taking what is ours into himself, *Yet not as I will, but as thou wilt*
(Mt 26:39).[18] And later St Paul, as though he denied himself and did
not have his own life, said: *It is no longer I who live but Christ who
lives in me* (Gal 2:20).

Do not be disturbed by what I have said. I have no intention of
denying free will. Rather I am speaking of a firm and steadfast disposition, a willing surrender,[19] so that from the one from whom we
have received being we long to receive being moved as well. It is like
the relation between an image and its archetype. [1076C] A seal con-
forms to the stamp against which it was pressed, and has neither
desire nor capability to receive an impression from something else,
or to put it forthrightly, it does not want to. Since it lays hold of God's
power or rather becomes God by divinization and delights more in
the displacement of those things perceived to be naturally its own.

[18]This text will become the basis for Maximus's later discussion of the question
of the two wills of Christ. On Maximus's interpretation of this passage see in particular *Opusculum* 6 (PG 91:65A–68D), translated below, pp. 173–76; also the study by
François-Marie Léthel, *Théologie de l'agonie du Christ.*

[19]The Greek expression (ἐκχώρησις γνωμική) is difficult to translate. Sherwood
renders it "voluntary outpassing," by which he means a "voluntary handing over of
our self-determination to God." This passing out of ourselves, however, does not
mean the destruction of the will "but its perfect fulfilment according to the capacity
of its nature" (Sherwood, *St. Maximus the Confessor,* ACW 21, p. 59). Maximus wishes
to say that when one is firmly attached to the good there is a voluntary transcending
of oneself, a giving over of oneself, a "willing surrender" in our translation, in which
one passes over into the deifying activity of God. In this "willing surrender" free will
is not eliminated but reaches its proper end in God. It is a "gnomic" (as opposed to
"natural") volition, i.e., one undertaken on the basis of moral experience. "I did not
do away with the natural activity of those who undergo this experience," writes Maximus, "as though its natural activity had ceased.... But I did show that the power that
is beyond being is alone capable of bringing about deification in those who by grace
are deified" (*Opusc.* 1, PG 91:33D–36A). For discussion see Sherwood, *The Earlier
Ambigua,* pp. 128–37; Thunberg, *Microcosm and Mediator,* pp. 218, 424, 427; and
Larchet, *La divinisation de l'homme,* p. 537.

Through the abundant grace of the Spirit it will be shown that God alone is at work, and in all things there will be only one activity,[20] that of God and of those worthy of kinship with God. God will be *all in all* wholly penetrating all who are his in a way that is appropriate to each (cf 1 Cor 15:28).

It is absolutely necessary that everything will cease its willful movement toward something else when the ultimate beauty that satisfies our desire appears. [1076D] In so far as we are able we will participate without being restricted, as it were, being uncontainably contained. All our actions and every sublime thought will tend eagerly towards that end "in which all desire comes to rest and beyond which they cannot be carried. For there is no other end towards which all free movement is directed than the rest found in total contemplation by those who have reached that point," as our blessed teacher says.[21] For nothing besides God will be known, nor will there be anything opposed to God that could entice one to desire it. [1077A] Instead, when God's ineffable majesty is made known, all intellectual and sensible things will be encompassed by him. It is like the light from the stars. The stars do not shine in the day. When the greater and incomparable light of the sun appears, they are hidden and cannot be seen by the senses. With respect to God this is even more so, for God is infinite, and uncreated things cannot be compared to created things.

When we learn the essential nature of living things, in what respect, how, and out of what they exist, we will not be driven by desire to know more. For if we know God our knowledge of each and everything will be brought to perfection, and, [1077B] in so far as possible, the infinite, divine and ineffable *dwelling place* (Jn 14:2) will be ours to enjoy. For this is what our sainted teacher said in his famous philosophical aphorism: " 'Then we shall know as we are known' (1 Cor 13:12), when we mingle our god-formed mind and

[20]The term here is ἐνέργεια and Maximus was later to retract the expression "one energy" because of its monergistic implications. See *Opusc.* 1 (PG 91:33A–B).

[21]Gregory Nazianzen, *Oration* 21.1.

divine reason to what is properly its own and the image returns to the archetype for which it now longs."[22]

Enough, then, with this foolishness of a non-existent henad! Drawing on the sense of the words and ideas in the Scriptures we have set forth what can be said about the ultimate condition that will one day prevail. Now it is time to discuss, with God's help, how we as portions of God have "slipped down" from God.

II

[1077C] If by reason and wisdom a person has come to understand that what exists was brought out of non-being into being[23] by God, if he intelligently directs the soul's imagination to the infinite differences and variety of things as they exist by nature and turns his questing eye with understanding towards the intelligible model (λόγος) according to which things have been made, would he not know that the one Logos is many *logoi*?[24] This is evident in the incomparable differences among created things. For each is unmistakably unique in itself and its identity remains distinct[25] in relation to other things. He will also know that the many *logoi* are the one Logos to whom all things are related and who exists in himself without confusion, the essential and individually distinctive God, the Logos of God the Father. He is the beginning and cause of all things *in whom all things were created, in heaven and on earth, visible and invisible, whether thrones or dominions or principalities* [1080A] *or authorities—all things were created from him and through him and for*

22Gregory Nazianzen, *Oration* 28.17.

23This phrase is repeated at 1085A.

24On this point see I.-H. Dalmais, "La théorie des 'logoi' des créatures chez S. Maxime le Confesseur," *Revue des sciences philosophiques et théologiques* 36 (1952): 244–49.

25The word in Greek is ἀσύγχυτος, "without confusion," one of the key terms used in the decree of the Council of Chalcedon in A.D. 451 to define the relation between the divine and human in Christ, who is "acknowledged in two natures *without confusion*, without change, without division, without separation."

him (Col 1:15–17; Rom 11:36). Because he held together in himself the *logoi* before they came to be, by his gracious will he created all things visible and invisible out of non-being.[26] *By his Word and by his Wisdom he made all things*[27] and is making all things, universals as well as particulars, at the proper time.

For we believe that a *logos* of angels preceded their creation, a *logos* preceded the creation of each of the beings and powers that fill the upper world, a *logos* preceded the creation of human beings, a *logos* preceded everything that receives its becoming from God, and so on. It is not necessary to mention them all. The Logos whose excellence is incomparable, ineffable and inconceivable in himself is exalted beyond all creation and even beyond the idea of difference and distinction. [1080B] This same Logos, whose goodness is revealed and multiplied in all the things that have their origin in him, with the degree of beauty appropriate to each being, *recapitulates all things in himself* (Eph 1:10). Through this Logos there came to be both being and continuing to be, for from him the things that were made came to be in a certain way and for a certain reason, and by continuing to be and by moving, they participate in God. For all things, in that they came to be from God, participate proportionally in God, whether by intellect, by reason, by sense-perception, by vital motion, or by some habitual fitness, as the great and inspired Dionysius the Areopagite thought.[28] Consequently, each of the intellectual and rational beings, whether angels or human beings, through the very Logos according to which each was created, who is in God and is "with God" (Jn 1:1), is "called and indeed is"[29] a "portion of God" through the Logos that preexisted in God as I have already argued.

[26]On the *logoi* see Pseudo-Dionysius, *Divine Names* 5.8 (PG 3:824C); also Augustine, *De diversis quaestionibus* 1.46.2 (PL 40:30).

[27]*O God of my fathers and Lord of mercy, who hast made all things by thy word, and by thy wisdom has formed man . . .* (Wis 9:1–2).

[28]See Pseudo-Dionysius, *Divine Names* 5.5–7 (PG 3:820A–821C).

[29]Maximus's phraseology *we are and are called* comes from 1 John; *we are and are called children of God* (1 Jn 3:1). See also below, 1081C and 1084C.

[1080C] Surely then, if someone is moved according to the Logos, he will come to be in God, in whom the *logos* of his being pre-exists as his beginning and cause. Furthermore, if he is moved by desire and wants to attain nothing else than his own beginning, he does not flow away from God. Rather, by constant straining toward God, he becomes God and is called a "portion of God" because he has become fit to participate in God. By drawing on wisdom and reason and by appropriate movement he lays hold of his proper beginning and cause. For there is no end toward which he can be moved, nor is he moved in any other way than toward his beginning, that is, he ascends to the Logos by whom he was created and in whom all things will ultimately be restored.[30] Clearly one's movement toward the divine reaches its end only when one reaches God.

[1080D] St Basil makes this clear in his interpretation of the holy prophet Isaiah when he writes: "*The true Sabbaths are the rest laid up for the people of God* (Heb 4:9). God can *bear these sabbaths*[31] because they are true. And the one *in which the world is crucified* (Gal 6:14) reaches these sabbaths of rest because he has clearly turned away from worldly things and returned to his own spiritual resting place. The one who arrives there will no longer be moved from his place, for there he finds quiet and tranquility."[32]

[1081A] Hence God is the place for all who are worthy of such happiness, as it is written: *Be thou a rock of refuge for me O God, and a place of refuge to save me* (Ps 31:2).[33] The *logoi* of all things known by God before their creation are securely fixed in God. They are in him who is the truth of all things. Yet all these things, things present

---

[30]Cf Acts 3:21. The Greek term is ἀποκατάστασις and refers to the restoration of all things to their original condition. It gained currency through the writings of Origen and was used by Gregory of Nyssa. For discussion of the idea in Maximus, see Polycarp Sherwood, *The Earlier Ambigua*, pp. 205–22.

[31]See Isaiah 1:13: *I cannot bear your new moons and your sabbaths.*

[32]Pseudo-Basil, *Commentary on Isaiah* 1:13 (PG 30:177C–D). This commentary, though traditionally attributed to St Basil of Caesarea, is generally thought to be the work of another writer.

[33]*House of refuge to save me* is the Septuagint rendering of Ps. 31:2.

and things to come, have not been brought into being contempora-
neously with their being known by God; rather each was created in
an appropriate way according to its *logos* at the proper time according to the wisdom of the maker, and each acquired concrete actual
existence in itself. For the maker is always existent Being, but they
exist in potentiality before they exist in actuality. [1081B]. It is impossible for the infinite to exist on the same level of being as finite
things, and no argument will ever be capable of demonstrating that
being and what is beyond being are the same, nor that the measured
and immeasurable can be put in the same class, nor that the absolute
can be ranked with that which exists in relation to other things, nor
that that which has nothing predicated of it and that which is constituted by predication belong together. For all created things are
defined, in their essence and in their way of developing, by their own
logoi and by the *logoi* of the beings that provide their external context. Through these *logoi* they find their defining limits.[34]

We are speechless before the sublime teaching about the Logos,
for He cannot be expressed in words or conceived in thought.
Although he is is beyond being and nothing can participate in him
in any way, nor is he any of the totality of things that can be known
in relation to other things, nevertheless we affirm that the one Logos
is many *logoi* and the many *logoi* are One. [1081C] Because the One
goes forth out of goodness into individual being, creating and preserving them, the One is many. Moreover the many are directed
toward the One and are providentially guided in that direction. It is
as though they were drawn to an all-powerful center that had built
into it the beginnings of the lines that go out from it and that gath-
ers them all together. In this way the many are one.[35] Therefore "we

---

[34]Cf *Amb.* 15 (PG 91:1217A–B): "All beings, by the *logos* by which they were
brought to being and exist, are perfectly firm and immovable; by the *logos* of things
seen as related to them, by which the ordering (οἰκονομία) of this universe is clearly
held together and conducted, all things move and admit of instability."

[35]See Pseudo-Dionysius the Areopagite: "The first gift therefore of the absolutely
transcendent Goodness is the gift of being, and that goodness is praised from those
that first and principally have a share of being. From it and in it are Being itself, the

are and are called"³⁶ a "portion of God" because the *logoi* of our
being pre-existed in God. Further, we are said "to have slipped down
from above" because we do not move in accord with the Logos (who
preexisted in God) through whom we came to be.

One who has learned to think devoutly about the *logoi* of existing things can explain this matter in another way. [1081D] There can
be no doubt that the one Word of God is the substance of virtue in
each person. For our Lord Jesus Christ himself is the substance of all
the virtues, as it is written: *This one God made our wisdom, our justice, our sanctification and redemption* (1 Cor 1:30). These things of
course are said about him absolutely, since he is wisdom and righteousness and sanctification itself. They are not, as in our case, simply attributed to him, as for example in the expression, a "wise man"
or a "just man."³⁷ It is evident that every person who participates in
virtue as a matter of habit unquestionably participates in God, the
substance of the virtues. [1084A] Whoever by his choices cultivates

source or beings, all beings and whatever else has a portion of existence. This characteristic is in it as an irrepressible, comprehensive, and singular feature. Every number
preexists uniquely in the monad and the monad holds every number in itself singu-
larly. Every number is united in the monad; it is differentiated and becomes plural
only insofar as it goes forth from this one. All the radii of a circle are brought together
in the unity of the center which contains all the straight lines brought together within
itself. These are linked one to another because of this single point of origin and they
are completely unified at this center. As they move a little away from it they are differentiated a little, and as they fall farther they are farther differentiated. That is, the
closer they are to the center point, the more they are at one with it and at one with
each other, and the more they travel away from it the more they are separated from
each other" (*Divine Names* 5.6, PG 3:820D–821A; trans. Luibheid, *Pseudo-Dionysius:
The Complete Works*, pp. 99–100).

    ³⁶1 Jn 3:1. See note 29 above.

    ³⁷On Maximus's interpretation of 1 Cor 1:30 see Origen: "Justice itself, essential
justice is Christ *whom God made our wisdom, our justice, our sanctification, and
redemption*. The justice in each person, however, is formed from that justice, so that
many kinds of justice come into existence in those who are saved; wherefore it has
also been written, *The Lord is justice and has loved justice* (Ps 10:7)" (*Commentary on
John 6:40*). Also Gregory of Nyssa: "It seems to me that through the ideas of virtue
and justice the Lord proposes himself to the desire of his hearers. For he became for
us wisdom from God, justice, sanctification and redemption. . . ." (*Homilies on the
Beatitudes* 4, GNO 7, pt. 2:122).

the good natural seed shows the end to be the same as the beginning and the beginning to be the same as the end. Indeed the beginning and the end are one.[38] As a result, he is in genuine harmony with God, since the goal of everything is given in its beginning and the end of everything is given in its ultimate goal. As to the beginning, in addition to receiving being itself, one receives the natural good by participation: as to the end, one zealously traverses one's course toward the beginning and source without deviation by means of one's good will and choice. And through this course one becomes God, being made God by God. To the inherent goodness of the image is added the likeness (cf Gen 1:26)[39] acquired by the practice of virtue and the exercise of the will.[40] The inclination to ascend and to see one's proper beginning was implanted in man by nature.

In such a person the apostolic word is fulfilled: [1084B] *In him we live and move and have our being* (Acts 17:28). For whoever does not violate the *logos* of his own existence that pre-existed in God *is* in God through diligence; and he *moves* in God according to the logos of his well-being that pre-existed in God when he lives virtuously; and he *lives* in God [41]according to the *logos* of his eternal being that pre-existed in God. On the one hand, insofar as he is already irrevocably one with himself in his disposition, he is free of unruly passions. But in the future age when graced with divinization, he will affectionately love and cleave to the *logoi* already mentioned that pre-existed in God, or rather, he will love God himself, in whom

[38]Cf Origen's comment on the end or consummation of all things: "The end is always like the beginning. Therefore, as there is one end of all things, so one must understand that there must be one beginning of all things; and as there is one end of many things, so from one beginning there arose many differences among things and kinds of things which through the goodness of God, by being subject to Christ and united with the Holy Spirit, are restored to one end which is like the beginning" (*On First Principles* 1.6.2).

[39]On the distinction between image and likeness in Maximus see Thunberg, *Microcosm and Mediator*, pp. 120–129.

[40]See *Chapters on Love* 3.25.

[41]On life with God as the ultimate goal of human life, see Augustine: "Why should human fraility hesitate to believe that we will one day live with God?" (*Sermon* 208c.1).

the *logoi* of beautiful things are securely grounded. In this way he becomes a "portion of God," insofar as he exists through the *logos* of his being which is in God and insofar as he is good through the *logos* of his well-being [1084C] which is in God; and insofar as he is God through the *logos* of his eternal being which is in God, he prizes the *logoi* and acts according to them.[42] Through them he places himself wholly in God alone, wholly imprinting and forming God alone in himself, so that by grace[43] he himself "is God and is called God."[44] By his gracious condescension God became man and is called man for the sake of man and by exchanging his condition for ours revealed the power that elevates man to God through his love for God and brings God down to man because of his love for man. By this blessed inversion, man is made God by divinization and God is made man by hominization.[45] [1084D] For the Word of God and God wills always and in all things to accomplish the mystery of his embodiment.

[42]"Of all things that do exist or will exist substantially . . . the *logoi*, firmly fixed, pre-exist in God, in accordance with which all things are and have become and abide, ever drawing near through natural motion to their purposed *logoi*. These things are rather constrained to being and receive, according to the kind and degree of their elective movement and motion, either well-being because of virtue and direct progress in regard to the *logos* by which they are, or well being because of the vice and motion out of harmony with the *logos* by which they exist. Or, to put it concisely: according to the having or the lack, in their natural participative faculty of him who exists by nature completely and unparticipated and who proffers himself entire simply and graciously by reason of his limitless goodness to all, the worthy and the unworthy, producing the permanence of everlasting being as each man of himself has been and is then disposed. For these the respective participation or non-participation of the very being, well-being and ever-being is the increase and augment of punishment for those not able to participate and of enjoyment for those who able to participate" (*Amb.* 42, PG 91:1329A–B).

[43]Cf *Ad Thal.* 60 (CCSG 22, 2:79, 117–120): "For truly he who is the Creator of the essence of created beings by nature had also to become the very Author of the deification of creatures by grace, in order that the Giver of well-being (τὸ εὖ εἶναι) might appear also as the gracious Giver of eternal well-being (τὸ ἀεὶ εὖ εἶναι)."

[44]Cf 1 Jn 3:1. See note 29 above.

[45]Maximus here reflects an expression in Gregory Nazianzen: "I became God to the extent that [God] became man" (*Oration* 29.19). See also Maximus, *Amb.* 60 (PG 91:1085B): man "becomes God to the extent that God became man."

Since each person is a "portion of God" by the *logos* of virtue in him, as the argument has shown, whoever abandons his own beginning and is irrationally swept along toward non-being is rightly said to have "slipped down from above", because he does not move toward his own beginning and cause according to which and for which and through which he came to be. He enters a condition of unstable gyrations and fearful disorder of soul and body, and though his end remains in place, he brings about his own defection by deliberately turning to what is worse. [1085A] Keeping these things in mind the phrase "to slip down" can be understood properly. It means that someone who had the ability to direct the steps of his soul unswervingly toward God voluntarily exchanged what is better, his true being, for what is worse, non-being.

III

With examples from Scripture St Dionysius the Areopagite teaches us to call these *logoi* "predeterminations" and "products of the divine will."[46] Similarily the disciples of Pantaenus, who was the teacher of the great Clement who wrote the *Miscellanies*, said that it is in keeping with Scripture to call them "products of the divine will."[47] Moreover when Christians were asked by some outsiders puffed up with their learning, how they can claim God knows existent things (which these critics had assumed), [1085B] and that he knows intellectual beings intellectually and sensible things sensibly, they replied that he neither knows sensible things sensibly nor intellectual things intellectually.[48] For it is out of the question that the one who is beyond

[46]See *Divine Names* 5.8. The Greek here is simply "divine wills." The translation "products of the divine will" comes from Brian Daley's forthcoming translation of von Balthasar's *Cosmic Liturgy*.

[47]See O. Staehlin, ed., *Clemens Alexandrinus*, GCS 3 (Leipzig: J. C. Hinrichs, 1905), lxv.

[48]This may come from Clement's work *On Providence* (GCS 3:224). See also J. Draeseke, "Zu Maximus Confessor," *Zeitschrift für wissenschaftliche Theologie* 47 (1904): 250–259.

existent things should know things in the manner proper to beings. But we say that God knows existent things as the products of his own acts of will, as the following argument will show.

If God made all things by his will[49] (which no one denies), and it is always pious and right to say that God knows his own will, and that he made each creature by an act of will, then God knows existing things as he knows the products of his own will, since he also made existing things by an act of will. Furthermore, I think that these assertions are in accord with what is said in the Scripture to Moses: *I know you above all* (Ex 18:11). And about some it was said: *The Lord knows those who are His* (2 Tim 2:19). [1085C] And to others he said: *I do not know you* (Mt 7:23; 15:12). Voluntary movement, either in accord with the will and word of God or against the will and word of God, prepared each person to hear the divine voice.

It is such things, I believe, that this saintly man meant when he said: "For then we will mingle our god-formed mind and our divine reason with what is properly its own and the image will return to the archetype it now longs for."[50] In a few words he attempts to dissuade those who hold these things from thinking that any being has at one time reached this point, [1085D] and explains in what sense we are a "portion of God." He also hints at the future possession of this blessed state and urges on those who are purified by hope and who yearn to enjoy it always, securely and unfailingly. For he knew that if we progress in a straight course, [1088A] led by reason and by nature toward that which has been impressed on our being by the Logos, as far as possible, without any searching whatsoever (for only in searching is there the possibility of stumbling and going wrong), we too will know things in a godlike way. No longer will we out of ignorance hold fast to the movement that envelops everything, but our mind and reason and spirit will advance to the great Mind, Logos

[49]Cf Rev 4:11.
[50]Gregory Nazianzen, *Oration* 28.17. This passage was already cited at 1077B.

and Spirit,[51] indeed our entire self will wholly pass over to God as an image to its archetype.

In his *Oration on Hail* Gregory taught something similar when he said: "They will be welcomed by the ineffable light and will contemplate the holy and majestic Trinity that shines clearly and brightly and unites itself wholly to the entire soul. This alone I take to be the kingdom of heaven"[52]—and here I dare add my words to his—[1088B] this will take place when every rational creature, whether angels or human beings, is filled with delight over spiritual pleasures, and has not carelessly corrupted the divine *logoi* which by nature were inclined towards the end set for them by the Creator. Instead they have kept themselves wholly chaste and steadfast, confident in the knowledge that they are to become instruments of the *divine nature* (cf 2 Pet 1:3–4). The fullness of God permeates them wholly as the soul permeates the body, and they become, so to speak, limbs of a body, well adapted and useful to the master. He directs them as he thinks best, filling them with his *own glory* (cf 2 Pet 1:3) and blessedness, and bestows on them unending life beyond imagining and wholly free from the signs of corruption that mark the present age. [1088C] He gives them life, not the life that comes from breathing air, nor that of veins coursing with blood, but the life that comes from being wholly infused with the fullness of God. God becomes to the soul (and through the soul to the body) what the soul is to the body, as God alone knows, so that the soul receives changelessness and the body immortality; hence the whole man, as the object of divine action, is divinized by being made God by the grace of God who became man. He remains wholly man in soul and body by nature, and becomes wholly God in body and soul by grace and by the unparalleled divine radiance of blessed glory appropriate to him. Nothing can be imagined more splendid and lofty than this.

For what is more desirable to God's precious ones than to be divinized, that is for God to be united with those who have become

[51]Maximus is thinking of the Holy Trinity.
[52]*Oration* 16.9 (*On his Father's Silence during the Plague of Hail*).

gods and by his goodness to make everything his own. Hence the
state that comes from contemplating God and enjoying the gladness
it gives is rightly called pleasure, rapture and joy. [1088D] It is called
pleasure because the term means that for which we naturally strive;
rapture, because it is an active receptivity by which what has received
power from without becomes itself capable of generating power that
is effective beyond itself, as in the previous examples of light permeating air and fire suffusing iron. [1089A] For God's precious ones
are persuaded that in truth human nature is given no loftier goal.
When it is achieved by necessity it brings with it impassibility. It is
called joy because it has nothing to gainsay it, neither from the past
nor from the future. For it is said that joy is neither conscious of past
sorrow nor has any place for that satiety that inevitably disappoints,
one reason why satiety is anticipated with trepidation. It is the same
with pleasure. Therefore, as the inspired Scriptures and our fathers,
who are wise from hearing the Scriptures read in the divine mysteries, confirm, "joy" is the most appropriate term to refer to the life
that is to come.[53]

Though the discussion has only skimmed the surface and my
abilities are limited, I have tried to show by arguments from reason,
from the Scriptures and from the Fathers, that none of the created
things that move has ever come to rest, nor obtained the prize laid
up in God's plan. It is impossible that those who have found the stability that comes from having their dwelling place (cf Jn 14:2) in God
will turn way from God. [1089B] How can those who have actually
found rest in God become satiated and be drawn away recklessly by
desire. For by definition, satiety quenches appetite. To demonstrate
this let me briefly offer an argument from reason.

Satiety comes about in two ways: either appetite is quenched
because it desired things that are trivial, or because it becomes nau-
seous by being drawn to what is base and repugnant. In the latter
case desire turns into loathing. But for those who enjoy fellowship

[53]See, e.g., Mt 25:21: Jn 16:20–24.

with God who is infinite and beautiful, desire becomes more intense and has no limit.

If this is so, as has already been demonstrated, there was no single entity (ἑνάς) of rational beings, that became satiated with its abode in God, then was divided, [1089C] and by its scattering brought about the origin of the world. Let us then not make the Good finite and valueless, capable of producing satiety and bringing about a revolt among those whose desire it could not satisfy. It appears, however, that some vainly assert this, and what is more, falsely claim that our blessed father Gregory taught these things. For they hold not only that he thought that souls fell from their former life into bodies to be punished for evils they had previously committed, but they also attempt with sweet sounding words to mislead others into thinking this is so by appealing to their personal integrity. But their behavior is neither commendable nor holy. [1089D] Let us then put an end to their fantasies by reverently examining the thinking of our teacher from yet another angle.

I V

In the passage under discussion Gregory did not intend to explain how human beings came to be, [1092A] but why misery attends their lives. For he laments the wretchedness we experience in our bodies when he writes: "O how I am united with the body yet alien from it. What I fear I treat with the utmost care, and what I love I have come to fear," and so on.[54] In the course of this oration he puts a question to himself about the reason for the evils that hold us in their grip and explains the role of the most-wise providence in this matter, when he says: "What does Wisdom have in mind for me and what is this great mystery?" In what follows he gives his answer to the question: "Is it God's intention that we who are a portion of God and have slipped down from above should out of self importance be so

[54]Gregory Nazianzen, *Oration* 14.7 (PG 35:865C).

haughty and puffed up because of our dignity that we despise our Creator? Hardly! Rather we should always look to him in our struggle against the weakness of the body. Its very limitations should be a form of training for those in our condition."⁵⁵ [1092B]

Gregory is saying that out of God's great goodness human beings were composed of a soul and body. The rational and intellectual soul given to man is made in the image of its maker and through desire and intense love it holds fast to God and participates in the divine life. The soul becomes godlike through divinization, and because God cares for what is lower, that is the body, and has given the command to love's one's neighbor, the soul prudently makes use of the body. By practicing the virtues the body gains familiarity with God and becomes a fellow servant with the soul. God who dwells in the soul uses it as an instrument to relate to the body and through the intimate bond between body and soul makes it possible for the body to share in the gift of immortality. [1092C] The result is that what God is to the soul the soul becomes to the body, and the one God, Creator of all, is shown to reside proportionately in all beings through human nature. Things that are by nature separated from one another return to a unity as they converge together in the one human being. When this happens God will be *all in all* (1 Cor 15:28), permeating all thing and at the same time giving independent existence to all things in himself. Then no existing thing will wander aimlessly or be deprived of God's presence. For through the presence of God we are called *gods* (Jn 10:35), *children of God* (Jn 1:12), *the body* (Eph 1:23) and *members* (Eph 5:30) of God, even "portion of God." In God's purpose this is the end toward which our lives are directed. For this end man was brought into the world.

Our forefather Adam, however, used his freedom to turn toward what was worse and to direct his desire away from what had been permitted to what was forbidden. [1092D] It was in his power *to be united to the Lord and become one spirit with God or to join himself to a prostitute and become one body with her* (1 Cor 6:15–16). But Adam

⁵⁵*Oration* 14.7, the passage from Gregory that is the basis for this *Ambiguum.*

was deceived and chose to cut himself off voluntarily from God's happy end for him, preferring by his own free choice to be drawn down to the earth (cf Gen 2:17) than to become God by grace. Out of wisdom and love for mankind, [1093A] as befits his goodness, God who works out our salvation, fixed a punishment that is suitable to the irrational movement of our intellectual faculty. The punishment was death, which means that the capacity to render to God what is due God alone, to love him with all our mind, was destroyed. As a result it is only when we have been taught by suffering that we who love non-being can regain the capacity to love what is.

Further on in the oration Gregory makes this clear: "But it seems to me, for this reason none of the good things of this present life can be relied on. They are shortlived. The things we see, though made by the creative Logos and the wisdom that transcends all wisdom, are always changing, now one way and now another, [1093B] born upward and then downward. That is why it seems we are being played with. Before something can be laid hold of it flees and escapes our grasp. Yet there is purpose in all this, for when we reflect on the instability and fickleness of such things, we are led to seek refuge in the enduring things that are to come. For if life always went well, would we not become so attached to our present state, even though we know it will not last, and by deception become enslaved to pleasure? In the end we would think that our present life is the best and noblest, and forget that, being made in the image of God, we are destined for higher things."[56]

Further, in his *Oration to the Citizens*, Gregory says: "We are nothing in relation to the authentic and original wisdom. Yet through the irregularity and fluctuation of what is seen, God leads us to what is stable and enduring, and beckons us to seek him alone [1093C] and to be illumined by the beams of light that come from him. Through the irregularity of things that are seen and shift back and forth God directs us to those that are stable and enduring."[57]

[56] *Oration* 14.20
[57] *Oration* 17.4.

As I have already said, in the passage under discussion our teacher is not explaining the reason for the creation of mankind, but the reason for the misery that sin brought into our life after we were created. This should be evident to anyone who studies Gregory's divine writings carefully and diligently. He is explaining whence this condition came to be, for what reason, by whom and for whose sake. In short his words show that the fall into sin became the occasion for God in his wisdom to work out our salvation.

[1093D] In his *Oration on the Nativity*, where he discusses the mystery by which human beings came to be, Gregory makes clear the significance of what he said. "Intellect and the senses, once distinguished from one another, remained within their own limits, and bore the magnificence of the Creator-Word in themselves . . . Though they praised God's mighty words silently, they were piercing heralds (cf Ps 19:1–3). But the two had not yet mingled, because the mind and the senses had not been joined together. This mingling would be a mark of greater wisdom and God's extravagance in the creation of living things, but the abundance of God's goodness was not yet made known. Hence the Creator-Word, wishing to display this mingling and to produce a single living being with both intellect and sensation, invisible and visible, made man. [1096A] Taking a body from already existing matter and breathing life into it from himself (Gen 2:7), the Word fashioned an intellectual soul made in the image of God as a kind of second cosmos. He placed this marvelous creature, though weak in comparison to other animals, on the earth, like an angel he was able to worship God with the senses as well as the intellect," and so on.[58]

Gregory also wrote in the *Oration on the Lights*: "Since this is the way things are with the three persons,[59] or with the one God, the worship of God should not be limited to heavenly beings, but should include worshippers here below so that all things may be filled with the glory of God. For everything is of God. This is why man was

[58] *Oration* 38.11.
[59] The context of the passage is a discussion of the Holy Trinity. See *Oration* 39.12.

created by the *hand of God* (Isaiah 66:2) and was honored by being made in the image of God."[60]

Though I have spoken only briefly about how Gregory understood these words I think it sufficient to establish what he meant, unless of course one is hostile to these ideas and is interested only in a debate. [1096B] If someone still wants to argue about what the teacher meant when he called us a "portion of God," further discussion will be futile. I have already explained the matter from several different perspectives. But, in order to show that what has been said is faithful to the inspired words of the holy and blessed apostle Paul, who received the *wisdom hidden in God before the ages* (1 Cor 2:7), and illuminated in every way the dark life of men and dispersed the cloud of ignorance, it is enough to cite what he wrote to the Ephesians: *That the God of our Lord Jesus Christ, the Father of glory, may give you a spirit of wisdom and of revelation in the knowledge of him, having the eyes of your hearts enlightened,* [1096C] *that you may know what is the hope, to which he has called you, what are the riches of his glorious inheritance in the saints, and what is the immeasurable greatness of his power in us who believe, according to the working of his great might which he accomplished in Christ when he raised him from the dead and made him sit at his right hand in the heavenly places, far above all rule and authority and power and dominion, and above every name that is named, not only in this age but also in that which is to come, and he has put all things under his feet and has made him the head over all things for the church, which is his body, the fullness of him who fills all in all* (Eph 1:17–23).

[1096D] And later in the same epistle he writes: *And his gifts were that some should be apostles, some prophets, some evangelists, some pastors and teachers, to equip the saints for the work of ministry, for building up the body of Christ, until we all attain to the unity of the faith and of the knowledge of the Son of God, to mature manhood, to the measure of the stature of the fullness of Christ; so that we may no*

---

[60] *Oration* 39.13.

*longer be children, tossed to and fro and carried about with every wind
of doctrine,* [1097A] *by the cunning of men, by their craftiness in deceit-
ful wiles. Rather, speaking the truth in love, we are to grow up in every
way into him who is the head, into Christ, from whom the whole body,
joined and knit together by every joint with which it is supplied, when
each part is working properly, makes bodily growth and upbuilds itself
in love* (Eph 4:11–16).

I do not think further testimony is required for someone who
lives a devout life and accepts the revelation of the truth as it has
been believed by Christians. One clearly learns it from the following
expressions: We are his *members* and his *body,* and *the fullness of
Christ* of God who *fills all things in every way* according to the plan
hidden in God the Father before the ages. And we are being *recapitulated in him* through his Son our Lord Jesus the Christ of God.[61]

[1097B] The *mystery hidden from the ages* (Col 1:26) and from
the nations is now revealed through the true and perfect incarnation
of the Son and God. For he united our nature to himself in a single
hypostasis, without division and without confusion, and joined us
to himself as a kind of first fruits. This holy flesh with its intellectual
and rational soul came from us and is ours. He deemed us worthy to
be one and the same with himself according to his humanity.[62] For
we were predestined before the ages (cf Eph 1:11–12) to be in him as
members of his body. He adapted us to himself and knitted us
together in the Spirit as a soul to a body and brought us to the measure of spiritual maturity derived from his fullness. For this we were
created; this was God's good purpose for us before the ages. [1097C]
But this renewal did not come about through the normal course of
things, it was only realized when a wholly new way of being human
appeared. God had made us like himself, and allowed us to participate in the very things that are most characteristic of his goodness.

---

[61]In contrast to the two previous citations from Ephesians here Maximus provides a pastiche of phrases taken from the epistle: Eph 4:16, 13; 1:23; 3:9; 1:10.

[62]On the particularity of Christ and cosmic redemption see David Yeago, "Jesus
of Nazareth and Cosmic Redemption," pp. 163–94.

Before the ages he had intended that man's end was to live in him, and to reach this blessed end he bestowed on us the good gift of our natural powers. But by misusing our natural powers we willingly rejected the way God had provided and we became estranged from God. For this reason another way was introduced, more marvelous and more befitting of God than the first, and as different from the former as what is above nature is different from what is according to nature. [1097D] And this, as we all believe, is the mystery of the mystical sojurn of God with men. *For if,* says the divine apostle, *the first covenant had been blameless, there would have been no occasion for a second* (Heb 8:7). It is clear to all that the mystery accomplished in Christ *at the end of age* (Heb 9:26) shows indisputably that the sin of our forefather Adam at the beginning of the age has run its course.

The term "portion," then was properly used by our teacher[63] in the ways we have explained, and anyone who approaches this matter with an open mind [1100A] and does not try to be clever, will understand it as follows: in this passage "portion" means member. For if member is part of the body and part is the same as portion, then member is the same as portion. And if portion is the same as member, and the bringing together and composition of the members produces an organic body, and an organic body united to an intellectual soul gives us a complete human being, then it is correct to say that the soul or the body is a part or member of man. The body is an instrument of the intellectual soul of a man, and the whole soul permeates the whole body and gives it life and motion. At the same time the soul is not divided or enclosed in it, since the soul is simple and incorporeal by nature. It is wholly present to the entire body and to each of its members. [1100B] The body is of such a nature that it can make place for the soul by an inherent power that is receptive to the soul's activity. The soul tightly clasps the various members that receive it in the different ways proper to each member's way of maintaining the unity of the body. Approach then the great and ineffable

[63]Gregory Nazianzen, *Oration* 14:7, the passage cited at the beginning of this *Ambiguum.*

mystery that is the blessed hope of Christians with these things in mind. If one does not attempt to forge images of what is great and heavenly using trivial and earthbound things, one's thinking on these matters will be more discerning and subtle.

Away then with the foolish view that souls exist before bodies. We believe the Lord when he says that those raised in the resurrection will not be able to die, for on that day the one who is ultimately desirable will be fully revealed and we will participate in Him. [1100C] He says: "Whoever lives and believes in me shall never die"(Jn 11:26). If the soul were pre-existent, it would be impossible, as has already been shown, for it to be so radically changed that it could die. Let no one, then, depart from good sense and foolishly assert false opinions about the soul.

If the body and the soul are parts of man, as we have seen, it must be granted that as parts each necessarily bears a relation to something other than itself. It is only as they are related to each other that they have the whole predicated of them. Something that is always spoken of in relation to something else must have come into existence with the other. For the parts by coming together constitute the whole, and what each is in essence can be distinguished only in thought. Therefore since they are parts of man it is impossible for either the soul or the body to exist before the other or indeed to exist after the other in time. [1100D] If that were not the case the necessary relation each has to the other would be destroyed.

Further, if the soul is a species in itself before it is joined to the body, and the body is a species before it is joined to the soul, and each, soul to body and body to soul, by being joined to the other brings about an entity that is different from what each is in itself, then there are two possibilities. Either they undergo a change or what they become is what they are by nature. If it is because of undergoing something, what they undergo makes them into something they were not. Which is to say they were corrupted. But if what they become is what they are by nature, this will always happen because it is their nature. The soul would never cease being reincarnated, nor the body being reanimated. [1101A] In my view, however, this is not what happens. The constitution of the whole as a species has nothing to do with having undergone something nor with the natural power of the parts coming together with each other. Rather there is a simultaneous coming to be of the whole species with its parts. It is impossible for one species to change into another species without corruption.

But some say, because the soul exists and subsists after death and the dissolution of he body, the soul was able to exist and to subsist before the body. But their argument is not persuasive. For what one means by origin is not the same as what one means by essence. The former refers to whence something is, where it is and in relation to what it is, but the latter refers to what something is and how it is. If so, the soul, after it has come to be, always exists because of its being; but because it has come to be, it is not independent of other things and its condition is determined by whence it is and where it is and in relation to what it is. [1101B] For the soul, after the death of the body, is not simply called soul, but the soul of a human being, indeed the soul of a certain human being. Even after it has departed the body, the whole human is predicated of it as part of its species according to its condition. In the same way, although the body is by nature mortal, because of how it came to be, it is not an independent entity. For the body, after its separation from the soul, is not simply called body, but the body of a man, indeed the body of a certain man, even though it will decompose and be broken down into the elements of which it was composed. For like the soul it has the whole human being predicted of it as part of its species according to its condition.[64]

Therefore the human being is composed of soul and body, for soul and body are indissolubly understood to be parts of the whole human species. [1101C] Soul and body came into being at the same

[64]Maximus's thinking on the unity of body and soul is similar to that of Augustine who wrote: Bodies "are not for ornament or aid, as though simply external to the soul, but have to do with the very nature of man" (*De cura pro mortuis gerenda* 4.6)

moment and their essential difference from each other in no way whatsoever impairs the *logoi* that inhere naturally and essentially in them. For that reason it is inconceivable to speak of the soul and body except in relation to each other. It is only as they come together to form a particular person that they exist. If either existed before the other, it would have to be understood as the soul or the body of the one to which the other belongs. The relation between them is immutable.

But enough of these things. If this discussion has not strayed from the truth, the thanks goes to God. For by your prayers[65] God has led me to think rightly about these matters. If, however, the truth has escaped me in any way, you will be able to instruct me, because you have been inspired by God to know these things.

---

[65]Maximus's essay was addressed to John bishop of Cyzicus to whom Maximus's early *Ambigua* are addressed.

On How the Creator Brings Order out of the Chaos of Bodily Existence

(PG 91:1101D–1105B)

[1101D] From Gregory's same *Oration*: "So long as matter bears with it chaos, as in a flowing stream . . ."[1]

I think that the intent of Gregory's discourse at this point follows closely the thinking of the preceding chapter.[2] Having devoted as much of his discourse as possible to those infatuated with matter and the body, Gregory adds these statements so that whoever [1104A]

---

[1]Gregory Nazianzen, *Oration* 14.30 (*On Love for the Poor*) (PG 35:897B).

[2]Gregory's full statement in question here reads: "But whether the affliction they suffer comes from God is not clear so long as matter carries with it chaos, as in a flowing stream." As Polycarp Sherwood has observed (*The Earlier Ambigua*, pp. 29–30), Maximus sees this statement, like the one under discussion in *Amb.* 7 (see esp. section IV, PG 91:1089D–1096B; trans. above, pp. 65–9), as fitting into a larger explanation of how the evils associated with bodily existence have come about, not as punishment for the sins of pre-incarnate souls (as in the Origenist scheme), but as the result of the historical (Adamic) fall. Gregory's present statement raises the issue of the precise origins of material instability and corporeal mutability within God's providential economy. In the background is the vexed question, already addressed by Gregory of Nyssa and taken up once again by Maximus (who with Nyssa rejected the Origenist solution), of how such instability and mutability could be only an *effect* stemming from Adam's sin in paradise and not somehow an antecedent *cause* of that sin. Was Adam not a passible being before he lapsed? Did he at first dwell in a state of *virtuous* passibility (cf *Ad Thal.* 61, trans. below, pp. 131–43)? On the place of *Amb.* 8 in this larger debate, see Polycarp Sherwood, "Maximus and Origenism: ΑΡΧΗ ΚΑΙ ΤΕΛΟΣ," *Berichte zum XI. internationalen Byzantinisten-Kongress* III, 1 (Münich, 1958), pp. 1–27, and esp. pp. 16–21.

examines the saint's intention with proper piety can interpret it as
follows. Man came into being adorned with the God-given beauty
of incorruptibility and immortality, but, having preferred the shame
of the material nature around him over spiritual beauty, and in addition wholly forgotten the eminent dignity of his soul—or rather the
God who beautified the soul with divine form—he plucked a "fruit"
which, according to the divine decree that wisely administers our
salvation, was worthy of the deliberative will (γνώμη),[3] thus reaping
not only bodily corruption and death, and the liability and propensity to every passion, but also the instability (τὸ ἄστατον) and
inequality of external and material being, and the capacity and
proneness for undergoing change.

There are two possible explanations of how this came about.
One possibility is that God, at the very moment humanity fell,
[1104B] blended our soul together with our body on account of the
transgression, and endowed it with the capacity to undergo change,
just as he gave the body the capacity to suffer, undergo corruption,
and be wholly dissolved—as was evinced when God covered the
body with the garments of skins (Gen 3:21). This explanation
accords with the text of Scripture: *And the creature was made subject
to corruption, not willingly, but for the sake of him who subjected it in
hope* (Rom 8:20). The other possibility is that from the beginning
God, in his foreknowledge, formed the soul in the aforesaid way
because he foresaw the coming transgression, so that by suffering
and experiencing evil on its own, the soul would come to an aware-
ness of itself and its proper dignity, and even gladly embrace detach-
ment with respect to the body.

For the all-wise Provider of our life allows what we do by our
own impulses to be used, quite naturally and frequently, for our
correction, [1104C] In the case of us who frantically deal with
our impulsive acts amid the confusion and the disorder of which
those acts are both an object and a cause, our Provider guides the

---

1 the "gnomic" will in connection with human fallenness, see *Ad Thal.* 21
ed below, pp. 109–13).

irrational love (ἔρως) which, in the meantime, we have directed
toward present diversions, back to that which is beloved by nature.[4]
For there are three general ways by which, they say for our instruction, our passions are healed. Through each of the three, God renders a healing treatment of the self-directing evil vexation of the
passions, as he wisely sets the chaos (τὸ ἄτακτον) of matter in good
order (εὐτάκτως), according to the better plan which transcends us
and leads toward the beneficial outcome that God himself knows.
For we, from whom is demanded a satisfaction for the sins of our
predecessors, retain no trace of those sins in our memory, [1104D]
because of our ignorance; or perhaps it is also the case that when we
remember the correction required to compensate for those wrongs,
we repudiate the correction. Either then—because we are unwilling
or incapable of such correction, on account of our inbred disposition toward vice—we are purged of the weakness; or else we reject
the present and indwelling vice and learn in advance to anticipate
restraining future evil; or else one man sets forth an admirable
example of superior perseverance and pious courage for other
human beings, if indeed there were a man distinguished in intelligence and virtue, [1105A] and competent in himself to uncover,
through unwavering engagement in formidable struggles, the truth
which has meanwhile lay hidden.

Gregory is therefore advising those who can think of nothing
beyond this present life that they not put their confidence in bodily
health and in the course of affairs that "bears" [their material life]
along as in a "flowing stream," nor exalt themselves at the expense of
those who lack these things, so long as the present life endures and
they embrace its corruption, to which is related both mutability and
change; and so long as there is uncertainty that something will happen to them arising from both the inequality and disordered state of

---

[4]The conversion of irrational love (ἔρως), the soul's natural desire, to the true
Good, is a familiar theme in the Cappadocian Fathers and in Maximus himself, as is
the notion of the soul being converted, as it were, to its own inherent beauty, the
image of God.

their body and their external affairs. This is what Gregory means, I
think, by saying "so long as matter bears with it chaos . . ." instead of
"so long as this whole realm is subject to corruption and change." It
is his way of saying that we are clothed in the body of humiliation,
and likewise [1105B] we are subject to the manifold evils that arise
from it because of its inherent weakness; and rather than magnify-
ing ourselves over others in view of the inequality all around us, we
should by prudent consideration even out the disparity of our
nature, which in its own right is equal in honor, by filling others'
deficiencies with our own abundances.[5] Perhaps it is even the case
that the present inequality is allowed to prevail in order to display
 our inner rational capacity for preferring virtue above everything
else. For the change and alteration of the body and of things external are for all human beings one and the same thing—both a bearing (φέρουσα) and a being born along (φερομένη)[6]—which also
knows chaos and conductibility as its only stability and its only
security.

[5]Origen and later Origenists had answered the dilemma of the inequality of bodies, or disparity of corporeal conditions, among rational creatures by referring to the
severity of their pre-incarnate sin. Maximus has gleaned from Gregory Nazianzen a
corrective response. Bodily inequality (and mutability) is rather a fact of material life,
an evidence of the latent chaos of material creation out of which God is working, in
the lives of the virtuous, to bring about a blessed orderliness, a gracious equality. The
virtuous must, then, actively engage in the ministry of "equalizing," both by their own
internal discipline of their bodily passions, and by their extraverted acts on behalf of
those who are even more severely challenged by bodily infirmity or by the "chaos" of
the passions. Our "abundances"—embodied, paradoxically it seems, in our own acts
of humility—help to reconcile their "deficiencies."

[6]Maximus is alluding again to Nazianzen's own terminology of matter "bearing"
or "conducting" chaos along with it, as in a flowing stream.

On Jesus Christ and the "Three Births"

(PG 91:1316A–1349A)

[1316A] From Gregory's *Oration on Baptism*: "The Logos knew three births for us: bodily birth, birth through baptism, and birth through resurrection." In addition to these Gregory broaches [1316B] another birth when he explains the births as follows: "My Christ showed that he honored all these births in himself: the first by the original and vital inbreathing (cf Gen 2:7); the second by his incarnation and the baptism with which he was baptized; and the third by the resurrection of which he was the *first fruits* (cf 1 Cor 15:20, 23), as he became the *Firstborn among many brethren* (Rom 8:29), and so also deigned to become *Firstborn from among the dead* (Col 1:18)."[1]

How is it that, in what has just been quoted, this godly teacher of ours seems to have added superfluously to what he initially stated? For having spoken of the three births—the bodily birth, the one through baptism, and the one through resurrection—it is as if he forgets [1316C] and in an apparently excessive phrase adds a fourth birth, since he speaks of one "by the original and vital inbreathing." He did not originally mention this with the three births. So he seems to be adding to what he said when he speaks of a birth "by the original and vital inbreathing."

[1]Gregory Nazianzen, *Or.* 40.2 (PG 36:360C).

Now whoever with proper virtue comes within range of our great teacher, and has not deviated far from his astute knowledge of divinity, knows how he is speaking truthfully in what he says here. Insofar as I understand him, in the weakness of my meager intelligence, I do not think that he is superfluously adding a fourth birth; rather, this birth is complementary of the aforementioned bodily birth and explains the divine principles (λόγοι) and modes (τρόποι) pertaining thereto. He who, on account of the creaturely origin (γένεσις) of the first Adam, [1316D] accepted becoming a man, and who did not spurn human birth (γέννησις) on account of Adam's transgression, demonstrated by his creaturely origin that he was condescending to him who had fallen, and by his human birth that he was voluntarily emptying himself for him who stood condemned.[2] Through his creaturely origin, he took it on himself to become by nature the same (as Adam) in terms of the "vital inbreathing" of man, and on that basis, receiving as man what was created in the divine image, he persevered without selling out his freedom or compromising his sinlessness. On the other hand, through his incarnational birth, when, in the form of a servant, he voluntarily assumed the likeness of corruptible humanity (cf Phil 2:7), he willingly allowed himself to be made subject virtually to the same natural passions as us yet without sin (cf Heb 4:15); the sinless one became morally liable, as it were.[3]

For he is doubly identified by the two parts of which he is constituted: he has [1317A] perfectly become the New Adam, while

[2]For the same distinction between primary creaturely origin (γένεσις) and birth (γέννησις), see *Ad Thal.* 21 (CCSG 7:127, 5–18; 129, 36–42; translated below, pp. 109, 111). The former designates the original coming-into-being of humanity, whose creation included the divine "inbreathing" (Gen 2:7); the latter designates birth according to the physical restrictions of sexual procreation that are a consequence of the Adamic fall. In the discussion that follows here, Maximus continues to develop the christological significance of this distinction.

[3]Maximus's reasoning is clear enough: in his primary origin (γένεσις) as a human being, Christ was, by the *logos* of his human nature, one with Adam; yet in taking the flesh, undergoing birth (γέννησις) *without sin,* he assumed the *tropos* of a new, unprecedented human existence. See also *Amb.* 31 (PG 91:1276A–B).

bearing in himself the first Adam, and he is both of these at once, without diminution. For, in being formed as a human being, he condescended to what was by law the creaturely origin of Adam prior to his fall, and so assumed in his human nature impeccability through the divine "inbreathing," but not incorruptibility. On the other hand, when, in his voluntary abasement, he underwent the human birth punitively instituted after the fall, he assumed the natural liability to passions but not sinfulness. He became the New Adam by assuming a sinless creaturely origin and yet submitting to a passible birth.[4] Perfectly combining the two parts in himself in a reciprocal relation, he effectively rectified the deficiency of the one with the extreme of the other, and vice versa, by [1317B] causing his birth amid dishonor to save and renew his honorable creaturely origin and, conversely, by making his creaturely origin sustain and preserve his birth.

By the "extreme" of his honorable creaturely origin I am speaking of its incorruptibility,[5] the basis of his impeccability, while the extreme of his ignoble human birth is that sinfulness which is the basis of all passion and corruption. Now of course the Savior in his incarnation did not assume this sinful passion, and corruption; he took on their consequences,[6] and enabled his birth to save his creaturely origin, and paradoxically renewed the incorruptibility of his creaturely origin by his own suffering. On the other hand, he enabled his creaturely origin to preserve his birth by sanctifying the

---

[4]On Christ's incarnational descent and "abasement" (κένωσις) as the New Adam, see also *Amb.* 4 (PG 91:1041A–1045C).

[5]There is an apparent discrepancy here with Maximus's assertion a little earlier (1317A) that, in being formed as a human being, Christ assumed natural sinlessness (by the divine inbreathing) but *not* incorruptibility. A possible explanation is that earlier Maximus was only denying *bodily* incorruptibility, in keeping with the Church's repudiation of the heresy of aphthartodocetism (the teaching that Christ's human body, unlike ours, was physically incorruptible even before his resurrection), while here, speaking of the "extreme" or optimal perfection of his creaturely origin (γένεσις), he has in mind Christ's antecedent moral and spiritual incorruptibility.

[6]Cf *Ad Thal.* 42 (CCSG 7:285–289; translated below, pp. 119–22) on how Christ *became* consequential "sin," not actual "sin" (2 Cor 5:21). See also the Introduction above, pp. 35–6.

passibility of that birth with his own sinlessness. He accomplished these things in order to preserve in full the creaturely origin [1317C] which secured his human nature in its divinely perfect principle, and fully to liberate from [the bonds of] birth that same nature, fallen through sin, that it might no longer embrace the same means of procreation as all the rest of the animals of the earth.

Therefore, if you physically connect his creaturely origin, formation as a human being, and divine inbreathing with his incarnation and birth, you should distinguish them only conceptually, and you will find that for our great teacher Gregory, the alleged "fourth" birth merely complements the bodily birth, and that his own distinction is purely conceptual and should be understood as we have explained it. I am saying that the creaturely origin that we have considered is by nature the same as the superadded birth, proper to which is God's original and life-giving infusion.

[1317D] *An Interpretation of Gregory's Phrase: "The Logos knew three births for us"*

In short, if you wish to know precisely what our teacher is saying, you should investigate what is the cardinal causal principle (λόγος) of humanity's creaturely origin, which ever endures in its proper permanence. And you should investigate what is the mode (τρόπος), according to God's disciplinary economy, of Christ's birth on account of human sin, the goal of which is the correction of disciplined humanity and humanity's complete return to the true principle of its creaturely origin, such that humanity might clearly learn how God, in becoming man, was perfectly begotten both in terms of his creaturely origin and his birth, [1320A] and that it was indeed for humanity that Christ maintained the *logos* of the creaturely origin while also wisely restoring humanity's means of existing to its true *logos*.[7]

----

[7]Dumitru Staniloae's comment on this passage is quite circumspect: "St. Maximus here analyzes in more detail the relation between the antecedent principle

Investigate all this, and you will rightly marvel at our teacher's insight, how he conceptually distinguishes those things that are naturally connected so as to elucidate the full meaning of this supremely divine mystery that was hidden from us. For his conceptual distinction[8] between the "vital inbreathing" and the enfleshment itself is suggestive of the distinction between the *logos* of creaturely origin and the *tropos* of birth.

God took on himself both of these for our sake and thus renewed our nature, or better yet he created our nature anew, and returned it to its primordial dignity of incorruptibility through his holy flesh, born of our own flesh and animated by a rational soul. What is more, he generously provided our nature with the gift of deification, [1320B] which he could not possibly have failed to bestow since he was himself God incarnate, indwelling the flesh in the same manner that the soul indwells the body, that is, thoroughly interpenetrating it in a union without confusion. Within this union, like that of the soul and body, he accepted being revealed instead of remaining

(*logos*) of man's creation, which is his cause, and the mode (*tropos*) of human birth introduced because of the fall. Through God's pedagogical economy (punitive education), this mode is intended to guide man toward the principle of his creation, and toward the knowledge of this creation. Man must advance by enduring the trials that stem from sin and so too from his birth through carnal desire in order to attain to his final goal: complete restoration in the principle or cause of his creation. . . . Maximus thus ascribes a positive role to birth through carnal desire, contrary to platonizing Origenism. Man's 'creation' has been effected not by a fall from an existence in primordial unity, but by a positive action of God for the sake of human beatitude. But once he has sinned, man can no longer be saved by a retreat from his terrestrial existence, but by a progression from birth associated with desire, a development consisting of the work of purification from sin, so that he can attain a final goal which lies, not behind him, but before him—i.e., in accordance with the original principle of his nature, which came into existence by creation. For this reason even the Son of God accepted the mode of bodily birth, but from a body that was pure from its very beginning. Because he combined this mode of birth (γέννησις) with the principle of his created provenance (γένεσις), he has thus unified the mode of human birth with the principle of human creation for the sake of the economy of salvation." Translated from Staniloae's "Commentaires" on the *Ambigua*, French trans. by Aurel Grigoras, in Emmanuel Ponsoye, ed. and trans., *Saint Maxime le Confesseur: Ambigua* (Paris and Suresnes: Les Éditions de l'Ancre, 1994), pp. 494–5.

[8]Maximus is referring to his emphasis back in 1317C.

hidden, insofar as he became manifest and thereby left his own natural hiddenness.[9] And what could be more amazing than the fact that, being God by nature, and seeing fit to become man by nature, he did not defy the limits of either one of the natures in relation to the other, but instead remained wholly God while becoming wholly human? Being God did not hinder him from becoming man, nor did becoming man diminish his divinity. He remained wholly one amid both, since he preserved both natures, and was truly existent in both natures at once. [1320C] Given that the natural difference between the two essential parts admitted no mixing, he was not divided, and in view of the supreme unity of his person, he knew no confusion. Nor did he convert into the inferior nature and thereby lapse into non-being. Nor did he simply simulate the salvific economy in the form and appearance of the flesh, as if to fulfill it by assuming whatever else is considered to be of a subordinate existence except the subordination itself. Rather, he took on himself our human nature in deed and in truth and united it to himself hypostatically—without change, alteration, diminution, or division; he maintained it inalterably, by its own essential principle and definition.

Accordingly, as our great and holy instructor Gregory indicates, he even dignified our birth, and truly became man [1320D] by undergoing a human birth, in order to liberate us from the bonds of that birth; and furthermore from the law of growth whereby, because of our punishment for sin, we multiply with seed almost like the grass of the field; and further still from having a common mode of procreative birth with plants and unreasoning animals. Let us quote the great Ezekiel, seer of grand visions, mystagogue of divine realities, who instructs us in the reason for the current economy of human salvation, when he says to Jerusalem, *Thus says the Lord to*

[9]The analogy of the soul-body relation as descriptive of the union of natures in Christ was familiar to Maximus from his reading of Cyril of Alexandria, who had deployed it abundantly in his refutation of Nestorianism. See, e.g., Cyril's *On the Unity of Christ* (PG 75:1292A–B); also John McGuckin, *St. Cyril of Alexandria: The Christological Controversy: Its History, Theology, and Texts*, Supplements to *Vigiliae Christianae* 23 (Leiden: E. J. Brill, 1994), pp. 198–201.

Jerusalem: "Your root and your beginning (γένεσις) *are of the land of Canaan. Your Father was an Amorite and your* [1321A] *mother a Chettite. On the day you were born, you did not tie your umbilical cord, and you were not washed in water; nor were you salted with salt or wrapped in swaddling clothes . . . You were cast out upon the face of the field because of the deformity of your soul on the day you were born. And I passed by you and saw that you were defiled with your own blood, and I said to you, 'Let there be life from out of your blood. Multiply, for I have granted you to be like grass sprung from the field'* " (Ezek 16:3–7). Therefore the Lord came to liberate our nature by redeeming it from being condemned to procreating through seed like the grass of the field, and from depending on blood for our life like the rest of the animals, and by returning our nature to the primordial grace of incorruptibility. He came to make plain to our nature the very beauty for which it was created in the beginning and in which it was thoroughly secure. He came to trample the [1321B] wickedness into which, through deceit, our nature unnaturally fell at the instant it was created,[10] thus depleting its whole potential. He came to bind to himself the faculty of desire (of which the *umbilical cord* is a symbol), that it might take on a procreative disposition fixed and unalterable in the good; he came to *wash* it *in water*, or in other words, to cleanse it of the taints of ignorance by washing it in the ocean of knowledge bestowed by grace; he came to *salt* it *with salt*, and to *wrap* it *in swaddling clothes*, that is, to render its natural operation steadfast by the Spirit in the good for which it was created, and thereby to cleanse it of the decay of the passions, to inoculate it against them, and to bring it fully to completion by securing it in the *swaddling clothes*, as it were, of the principles of created beings.

---

[10]In *Ad Thal.* 61 (CCSG 22:85, 8–16), Maximus uses this same phrase—"at the instant he was created" (ἅμα τῷ γίνεσθαι)—to describe the immediacy of Adam's fall. It is a significant nuance, for he is trying to avoid the problems associated with an "extended" prelapsarian state (viz., how a being created in the enjoyment of original perfection could, having already experienced that enjoyment, nonetheless go on to abuse his faculties and incline toward evils mistaken as "apparent" goods). Fallenness has been the dilemma of humankind *virtually from the beginning.*

An Alternative Interpretation of the Same Phrase

But perhaps when he says that "the Logos knew three births for us," and [1321C] introduces the duality of principle and mode with respect to human origins, our teacher Gregory is distinguishing between soul and body, and thus making a conceptual distinction between two bodily births: that of the soul, ineffably constituted by the divine and life-giving infusion; and that of the body itself, which is constituted of the underlying matter of the body from which it takes existence the moment it is ensouled at conception.[11] For it is not legitimate to say that the principle and mode of origination are absolutely the same for both the soul and the body, since the two are not identical in essence with each other. For their being is not the same, and clearly the principle and mode of origination is different for each of them. Rather, it is correct to assume that the principle and mode of the soul—[1321D] according to which it comes into being, exists, and immutably endures while the body is conjoined with it— are different.

A Concise Reflection for Those Who Say that Souls Either Preexist or Post-exist Bodies

If they—soul and body, I mean—exist simultaneously, and come into being at the same time, neither one, as I have said,[12] preexisting or post-existing the other as far as their origin is concerned, lest either one be extricated from the [1324A] species that the two constitute, then truly the principle of relation maintains that each has its proper subsistence (ὑπόστασις) as a part of the one species. And the subsistence [of each] upholds wholly and completely the natural union of the one to the other. For this reason, then, the co-subsistence of the two according to a natural synthesis of one thing

---

[11]Again showing his anti-Origenism, Maximus is careful to ascribe to the soul only an *ontological*, not a *temporal*, priority to the body.

[12]Maximus is referring here to his extensive discussion of the coexistence of soul and body already in *Amb.* 7 (PG 91:1089D–1101C).

with another can never be complete without corrupting [either body or soul] and turning it into what it was not. For it would be unnatural for a preexisting thing, subsisting proper to itself, to be turned into the subsistence of a species of something else. But if in order to complete the species of another the preexisting thing admits of synthesis with another, the result is either wholly natural or unnatural. If natural, then it will never cease from synthesis with another thing in order to complete the other's species, due to the force of nature [1324B] from which it cannot be altered. It is for this reason that the soul is never conceived apart from the body, nor the body apart from the soul. The sophistry [of those who say that souls preexist or post-exist bodies] turns to what defies intelligence to the point of foolishness, forcing such sophists into the very thing they are diligent to avoid. But if it is contrary to nature that one of these two [soul or body] admits of synthesis with the other in order to complete the other's species, it is entirely corrupted by departing from its natural character, becoming what is unnatural for it to be, and so changing into what it was not. What could possibly be more absurd? But let us return to our original discussion.

[1324C] The soul, as our teacher Gregory clearly states, originates not from underlying matter, like bodies, but, ineffably and unknowably, from a divinely willed vital inbreathing comprehended only by the soul's Creator himself. The soul arises at conception simultaneously with the body to form one complete human being. The body, of course, is created from the underlying matter of another body at conception, and at once enters into synthesis with the soul to form one species with it. Our teacher makes this point even more clearly elsewhere with the phrase ". . . according to the double power of inbreathing, and we are all inbreathed with breath and with holy Spirit."[13] Thus we must distinguish intellectually at conception between, on the one hand, the vital inbreathing and [1324D] the Holy Spirit which underlie the noetic essence of the soul, and, on the other hand, the enfleshment and "breath" which

[13]Gregory Nazianzen, *Or.* 30.20 (SC 250:270, 35–36).

underlie the nature of bodies, as the Fathers say. Our progenitor
Adam came into being in a secret way, with a different principle of
his soul's being and a different mode of its generation, and obviously
a different principle and generative mode for his body as well. Holy
Scripture abundantly reveals this to us, and does not allow us to con-
fuse Adam's soul and body as naturally coinciding according to one
and the same mode of generation; nor does it allow us to know the
essential principle and mode of generation of either one.

[1325A] Granted, then, that for Adam there is a dual power of
inbreathing and that the two are concurrent at the beginning of his
existence, what might one say of the duality—of soul and body, I
mean—in the humanity of our God and Savior Jesus Christ? This
same union [of soul and body] in Christ retains as much resemblance as possible to that in the first Adam. For as our teacher himself says, the God who took [Adam's] body from what clearly was
newly finished preexistent matter, which he endowed with life from
himself (precisely what the Logos knew as an intelligent soul and the
image of God [Gen 1:26–27]), created humanity.[14] And in the same
way, the Creator of humanity was he who assumed his body from
the immaculate Virgin, as if from undefiled earth, and who, endow-
ing it with life from himself (what, again, the Logos knew as an intelligent soul and the image of God), fashioned his own humanity.
[1325B] Or rather, the Creator of humanity was he who, as almighty
and immutable, willingly for our sake fashioned his own manhood
at the time he took the flesh and animated it with an intelligent and
rational soul.

In my judgment at least, our teacher Gregory is saying that our
Lord and God has honored the three births that we ourselves undergo, that is to say, the three general modes of our origin in being (τὸ
εἶναι), in well-being (τὸ εὖ εἶναι), and in eternal being (τὸ ἀεὶ
εἶναι).[15] The first birth, in which we receive being itself, is bodily

[14]Here Maximus is referring to Gregory Nazianzen, *Or.* 38.11 (*On the Theophany*)
(PG 36:321C–324A).
[15]This is a familiar triad in Maximus (cf *Amb.* 7, PG 91:1073C, 1084B–C; *Amb.* 65,

birth, a single appearance of both together—soul and body—
according to their coexistence as parts simultaneous with each other,
distinguished as two only by the different modes of origin proper to
each. The second birth comes through baptism, in which we receive
well-being in abundance. The third birth comes through resurrection, in which [1325C] we are translated by grace unto eternal
well-being. So then it is necessary to scrutinize our teacher's words
precisely because of those who calumniate well-established truths.
For by dividing bodily birth within a single notion for the reason
given here, our teacher determines that at the one common moment
of his conception—not in some movement thought to happen in a
prior time—the Lord received the life-giving spirit, the infusion of
his humanity, or in other words, the intelligent soul appearing
simultaneously with his body born from the Virgin, and not after
conception....[16]

† † † † † †

*How Innovation Takes Place even as the Things Innovated Remain
Unaltered in their Nature*

[1341D] Generally speaking, all <u>innovation</u> (καινοτομία) is manifested <u>in relation to the mode</u> (τρόπος) <u>of the thing innovated</u>, not

1392A–B; *Chapters on Theology and Economy* 1.56, PG 90:1104C). It is discussed at
length by Thunberg, *Microcosm and Mediator*, pp. 368–73; Larchet, *La divinisation de
l'homme*, pp. 165–74; and von Balthasar, *Kosmische Liturgie*, pp. 622–3.

[16]At this point, Maximus enters upon two long excurses, the first directed against
those who hold that souls preexist bodies (1325D–1336B), the second against those
who argue that bodies preexist souls (1336C–1341C), both intended to vindicate the
principle of the *coexistence* of souls and bodies in the singular species (εἶδος) of
human nature. Maximus argues as well that the Logos incarnate has "innovated"
human nature not in its natural principle (λόγος φύσεως) but in its postlapsarian
"existential mode" (τρόπος ὑπάρξεως), inaugurated through his virginal conception
and birth (see 1341C; cf *Ad Thal.* 21). Our translation of *Amb.* 42 resumes with Maximus's discussion of the general character of creaturely "renewal," in which we again
see how his teleology, like his Christology, is integral to his cosmology and doctrine
of created natures.

its natural principle (λόγος). The principle, if it undergoes innovation, corrupts the nature, as the nature in that case does not maintain inviolate the principle according to which it exists. The mode thus innovated, while the natural principle is preserved, displays a miraculous power, insofar as the nature appears to be acted upon, and to act, clearly beyond its normal scope. The principle of human nature is to exist in soul and body as one nature constituted of rational soul and a body; but its mode is the scheme in which it naturally acts and is acted upon, which can frequently change and undergo alteration without changing at all the nature along with it. [1344A] Such is the case for every other created thing as well, when God, because of his providence over what he has preconceived and in order to demonstrate his power over all and through all things, desires to renew it with respect to its creation.

We see this precisely in the magnificence of miraculous signs and wonders that God performed from on high. God acted on this principle of innovation when he translated the blessed Enoch and Elijah from life in the flesh, subject to corruption, to a different form of life (2 Kg 2:11; Gen 5:24), not by altering their human nature, but by changing the mode and domain of action proper to their nature. He did the same when he made water engulf the wicked men who had established themselves on the earth in such great numbers, while enabling the first sailor Noah and the wild animals appearing with him in the ark to survive unharmed (Gen 6:5–8:22). He did the same when [1344B] he honored his great servants Abraham and Sarah with a son beyond their age, beyond the alleged limits and natural time of childbearing (Gen 17:15–17; 18:9–15; 21:1–7). He did the same when he rained down fire to consume the contrivers of impiety (Gen 19:24). Nothing was diminished at all so far as its natural principle was concerned. God set fire to the burning bush without it being consumed in order to call his servant (Ex 3:2), and gave water the quality of blood in Egypt (Exod 7:17) without denying its nature at all, since the water remained water by nature even after it turned red.

And the same is true of the rest of the signs and wonders God performed there to give the faithful the hope of liberation from overwhelming perils, and to give the unbelieving a taste of his punitive power so as to dissolve [1344C] the hardness toward God that kept coming upon them: when he divided the sea with the rod and kept the flow of the water apart, without violating its nature, in order to give passage to the pursued and to thwart those who ruthlessly pursue what is good and free (Ex 14:1–31); when he sweetened water with a tree (Ex 15:24–25); when he rained down from heaven a strange and unknown bread that had not been artificially prepared (Ex 16:1–8); when he suddenly produced an abundance of edible birds from the sea (Ex 16:13; Num 11:31–32)—all apart from the natural sequence of things—in order to console those who were distressed in the desert; when he proved the rock to be a "mother" of water in order to secure the faith of those who were deserting amid the struggles (Ex 17:1–7); when he drove back a river to give dry passage to a godly people (Josh 3:1–17); when he miraculously suspended the unhindered course of the sun and the moon, rendering immovable the perpetually moving nature of the encompassing heavens, [1344D] in order to destroy an impious army when it stupidly mounted opposition against God (Josh 10:12–14), and so that the power of these ancient spectacles might come to completion, and the sure and long-promised inheritance be possessed.

So too with any of the rest of the alleged divine deeds in the promised land and in as many lands as were left that ancient Israel entered when they transgressed (cf Josh 2:19–3:6), God performed these acts with respect to the mode of operation, not the principle of existence when innovating the nature of the things he renewed. In company with all of these achievements, and yet after them all, God fulfilled for our sake the truly new mystery of his incarnation, a mystery for which and through which all these other things took place. Here again, [1345A] God innovated human nature in terms of its mode, not its principle, by assuming flesh mediated by an intelligent soul; for he was ineffably conceived without human seed and truly begotten as perfect man without corruption, having an intelligent soul together with his body from the very same moment of his ineffable conception.

That Every Nature, by its Proper Principle, Always Has Its Own End (τέλος)

Generally speaking, no nature, intelligible and sensible, simple and composite, in any way at all ever receives the beginning of its existence from its parts; nor is it able to subsist as half of itself. If the nature is composite, however, [1345B] the perfect whole is constituted collectively of the complete parts proper to it, and there is no temporal hiatus (διάστημα) of any kind within the nature itself or among the reciprocal parts of which it is constituted. Similarly if the nature is simple, or intelligible, it is, as a complete whole, constituted of its perfect principles, and there is no temporal gap at all separating it from its own constitutive principles. For in general, there has never been, nor is there now, nor will there ever be any nature in created beings, subsisting according to its own principle, that is anything other than what it is at present; and it is not now or will it ever be in the future what it was not in the past. The principles of these natures have enjoyed perfection in God simultaneous with their very existence, and their creation and [1345C] substantiation are thoroughly incapable of admitting any addition to, or subtraction from, what the nature is in itself. But I think that this will suffice as a digression from our discourse and a present inquiry directed toward these [opponents of ours], to keep us from being easily dragged off into absurd opinions by those who try to turn the faith into a piece of skillful rhetoric based on clever arguments.

Why Does Our Teacher Connect the Birth through Baptism with the Incarnation?

To what purpose, and for what reason, does our teacher Gregory connect the birth through baptism with the incarnation? [1345D]

(I have heretofore left this issue aside for investigation). I will speak briefly and offer as much as I have been able to learn. Those who treat the divine oracles mystically, and who dignify them, quite appropriately, with more sublime speculations, say that in the beginning humanity was created in the image of God (Gen 1:26–27) in order to be perpetually born by the Spirit in the exercise of free choice (προαίρεσις),[17] and to acquire the additional gift of assimilation to God by keeping the divine commandment, such that man, as fashioned from God by nature, might become son of God and divine by grace through the Spirit.[18] For created man could not be revealed as son of God through deification by grace without first being born by the Spirit in the exercise of free choice, because of the power of self-movement and self-determination inherent in human nature.[19]

[1348A] Since the first man spurned this deifying, divine, and immaterial birth when he preferred what was delectable and obvious to his senses over intelligible and meanwhile invisible goods, he was justly condemned to a material, mortal, bodily birth outside the scope of his free choice. God deservedly punished him for willingly choosing morally inferior objects by replacing his free, impassible, voluntary, and chaste birth with a passible, servile, restrictive birth akin to that of the unreasoning and unintelligent beasts of the earth;

[17]On the Spirit's gracing of free choice (προαίρεσις) through baptism, see also *Ad Thal.* 6 (CCSG 7:69–71; translated below, pp. 103–4).

[18]Maximus here makes two important distinctions that he develops more substantially elsewhere. First is the distinction, appropriated from Origen (*De princ.* 3.6.1, GCS—Origenes Werke 5:280, 6–17), between the "image" (εἰκών) and "likeness" (ὁμοίωσις) of God (Gen 1:27–27) indicating respectively the protological endowment and the eschatological vocation of humanity (cf *Chapters on Love* 3.25, PG 90:1024B–C; *Questions and Difficulties* III,1, CCSG 10:170, 2–20; also Thunberg, *Microcosm and Mediator*, pp. 120–29). The second is the distinction of "nature" and "grace" which in Maximus's usage must not be confused with Western approaches to this same dialectic. For him, nature is already "graced" by its intrinsic openness to transformation, and is completed "sabbatically" in the transition to deification (cf *Chapters on Theology and Economy* 1.55, PG 90:1104B–C; 1.67, 1108B; *Chapters on Love* 3.25, PG 90:1024B–C; *Ad Thal.* 35, CCSG 7:241, 39–44; *Opusculum* 1, PG 91:33C–36A).

[19]Cf *Ad Thal.* 6 (CCSG 7:69).

and by replacing the divine and ineffable honor of dwelling with God with the dishonor of being put on a material par with mindless beasts.

[1348B] Desiring, then, to liberate humanity from such dishonor and to return humanity to its divine inheritance, the Logos who created human nature truly became a man, humanly begotten, and underwent a sinless bodily birth for humanity's sake; and he who is God by essence and Son of God by nature, voluntarily submitting himself for our sake to the birth leading to spiritual adoption, was baptized in order to annul bodily birth. Since, then, he who made us, he who alone shares divinity and glory with the Father and the Spirit, truly became for our sake a man like us, humanly begotten and bodily born yet without sin; and since, as God by nature, he also consented for our sake to undergo birth unto spiritual adoption through baptism, our teacher Gregory has, in my judgment, therefore connected the baptismal birth with the incarnation, [1348C] such that baptismal birth will be considered an annulment of, and liberation from, bodily birth. It was for freely spurning this (the birth by the Spirit leading to deification, I mean) that Adam was condemned to the bodily birth that leads to corruption. He, then, who in his goodness and philanthropy willingly became a man amid our transgression, voluntarily subjected himself to condemnation along with us; he who is alone truly free and sinless consented to a bodily birth in which lay the very power of our condemnation, and thereby mystically restored the birth in the Spirit.

And so for our sake loosing within himself the bonds of bodily birth, he granted us through spiritual birth, according to our own volition, power to become children of God instead of children of flesh [1348D] and blood if we have faith in his name (cf Jn 1:12–13). For the Savior the sequence was, first of all, incarnation and bodily birth for my sake; and so thereupon the birth in the Spirit through baptism, originally spurned by Adam, for the sake of my salvation and restoration by grace, or, to describe it even more vividly, my very remaking. God, as it were, connected for me the principle of my

being and the principle of my well-being, bridging the separation
and distance between them that I had caused, and thereby wisely
drew them together in the principle of eternal being. By this principle, it is no longer a matter of humanity bearing or being born along
existentially,[20] since in this respect the economy of visible things
comes to an end with the great and general resurrection [1349A]
wherein humanity is born into immortality in an unchanging state
of being. It is for this [principle of eternal being] that the nature of
visible things received its existence in the beginning; and by this
principle that same nature will acquire by grace the state of essential
incorruptibility.

But if it seems good to you, let us recall briefly the basic thrust
of what we have said and summarize. We consider the bodily birth
of our Savior to admit of a conceptual distinction between the
antecedent principle of his human nature and his actual existence
like us, in which state he died; and furthermore between the natural
principle of his creaturely origin and the mode of his birth; and
still further between the different modes of origin of soul and body
respecting the essence of each; and finally, in addition to these,
between non-sexual conception and birth without corruption. It is
your responsibility, then, as just critics, to judge what is superior
from the proposals set forth here.

[20]Maximus is implicitly referring here to the dialectic of activity ("bearing," τὸ
φέρειν) and passivity ("being born along," τὸ φέρεσθαι) inherent in material existence. He has already dealt with the bodily aspect of this dialectic in *Amb.* 8 (PG
91:1101D–1104B, translated above, pp. 75–8).

AD THALASSIUM 1

On the Utility of the Passions[1]

(CCSG 7:47–49)

Q. [47] Are the passions evil in themselves or do they become so when used in an evil way? I am speaking of pleasure, grief, desire, fear, and the rest.

R. These passions, and the rest as well, were not originally created together with human nature, for if they had been they would contribute to the definition of human nature. But following what the eminent Gregory of Nyssa taught,[2] I say that, on account of humanity's fall from perfection, the passions were introduced and attached themselves to the more irrational part of human nature. Then, immediately[3] after humanity had sinned, the divine and blessed image was displaced by the clear and obvious likeness to unreasoning animals.

---

[1]This question, the only one in the *Ad Thalassium* not focused on a specifically scriptural difficulty, naturally follows on the Introduction to this great work, where Maximus has already addressed Thalassius's keen interest in the roots and operations of the passions.

[2]See Gregory of Nyssa, *De virginitate* 12 (GNO 8, pt. 1:297, 24–300, 2); ibid. 18 (GNO 8, pt. 1:317, 10–319, 25); *De anima et resurrectione* (PG 46:49B–68A).

[3]Cf *Ad Thal.* 61 (CCSG 22:85, 13) and *Amb.* 42 (PG 91:1321B), where Maximus likewise uses the adverb ἅμα to describe the immediacy of Adam's abuse of his passible faculties: *at the instant he was created* (ἅμα τῷ γίνεσθαι). Maximus clearly wants to indicate that Adam's perfection, historically, was more a potency than an actuality, thereby avoiding any possible implication of a "double creation" of humanity (before and after the fall), as in the Origenist cosmology.

The passions, moreover, <u>become good</u> in those who are <u>spiritu-</u>
<u>ally earnest</u> once they have <u>wisely separated them from corporeal</u>
<u>objects</u> and <u>used them to gain possession of heavenly things</u>. For
instance, they can <u>turn desire</u> (ἐπιθυμία) <u>into the appetitive move-</u>
<u>ment of the mind's longing for divine things</u>, or <u>pleasure</u> (ἡδονή)
into the <u>unadulterated joy of the mind</u> when enticed toward divine
gifts, or <u>fear</u> (φόβος) into <u>cautious concern for imminent punish-</u>
<u>ment for sins</u> committed, or <u>grief</u> (λύπη) <u>into corrective repentance</u>
<u>of a present evil.</u> In short, we can compare this with the wise physi-
cians who remove the existing or festering <u>infection of the body</u>
using the poisonous beast, the viper. [49] ⟨The spiritually earnest⟩use
<u>the passions to destroy a present or anticipated evil, and to embrace</u>
and <u>hold to virtue and knowledge</u>.[4] Thus, as I have already suggested, the passions become good when they are used by those who
take every thought captive in order to obey Christ (2 Cor 10:5).[5]

What this means is that if Scripture mentions anything about
the passions in connection with God and the saints, the following
applies: in connection with God, the passions are mentioned for our
benefit, revealing the saving and beneficial movements of divine
providence accommodated in a way that befits our own experience;
with reference to the saints, on the other hand, when the passions are
mentioned it is because the saints cannot convey in corporeal speech
their spiritual inclinations and dispositions toward God apart from
human passions.

[4]Inspired particularly by Gregory of Nyssa, Maximus's doctrine of the good
"use" (χρῆσις) of the passions—passions which, if used well, serve the love of God
and "texture" the spiritual life—is a crucial component in the Confessor's overall
ascetical theology. See also Blowers, "Gentiles of the Soul: Maximus the Confessor on
the Substructure and Transformation of the Human Passions," especially pp. 68–73,
76–9; and Wilken, "Maximus the Confessor on the Affections in Historical Perspective," pp. 412–23.

[5]The reference here to Paul is hardly a casual prooftext, since it supports Maximus's conviction that the passions are not simply arbitrary movements of affection
but "thoughts"—however primitive—that operate within the domain of the mind
and indicate its deep-seated moral dispositions.

AD THALASSIUM 2

On God's Preservation and Integration of the Universe

(CCSG 7:51)

Q. If the Creator made all the forms which fill out the world in six days (cf Gen 1:31–2:2), what is the Father doing henceforth? For the Savior says, *My Father is working even now, just as I am working* (Jn 5:17). Is he therefore speaking of a preservation of what he had once created?[1]

R. God, as he alone knew how, completed the primary principles (λόγοι) of creatures and the universal essences of beings once for all. Yet he is still at work, not only preserving these creatures in their very existence (τὸ εἶναι) but effecting the formation, progress, and sustenance of the individual parts that are potential within them. Even

---

[1]Thalassius already anticipates the resolution of his own query, and Maximus will follow suit. The relationship between Gen 2:2 and Jn 5:17 was already well-established in patristic tradition, especially in the context of anti-Manichaean exegesis, where there was need to show how God's "rest" was only figurative, while his present "work" is but an ongoing preservation of his original creation: cf Pseudo-Archelaeus, *Acta disputationis cum Manete* 31 (PG 10:1476B–1477A); Augustine, *De Genesi contra Manichaeos* 1.22.33 (PL 34:189). Even in a non-polemical setting the same argument stood: e.g. Origen, *Hom. in Num.* 23.4 (GCS-Origenes Werke 7:215–216); Augustine, *De Genesi ad litteram* 4.11.21–4.12.22 (CSEL 28:107–109). As a christological testimony, Jn 5:17 was cited to affirm Christ's own activity in the preservation (συντήρησις) and economy (οἰκονομία) of God's good creation: e.g., Gregory Nazianzen, *Or. theol.* 4.11 (PG 36:117A–B).

now in his providence he is bringing about the assimilation of particulars to universals until he might unite creatures' own voluntary
inclination to the more universal natural principle of rational being
through the movement of these particular creatures toward well-
being (τὸ εὖ εἶναι), and make them harmonious and self-moving in
relation to one another and to the whole universe.[2] In this way there
shall be no intentional divergence between universals and particulars.[3] Rather, one and the same principle shall be observable
throughout the universe, admitting of no differentiation by the individual modes according to which created beings are predicated, and
displaying the grace of God effective to deify the universe.[4] It is on
the basis of this grace that the divine Logos, when he became man,
said, *My Father is working even now, and I am working.* The Father
approves this work, the Son properly carries it out, and the Holy
Spirit essentially completes both the Father's approval of it all and
the Son's execution of it,[5] in order that the God in Trinity might be

[2]Here, in effect, is a brief encapsulation of Maximus's entire christocentric cosmology: the binding of all particular beings, in their individual modes (τρόποι) of
existence, and with their peculiar drives and volition, to the universal whole as manifested in the λόγοι of all created things. On the divine providence pervading the cosmos, see also *Amb.* 10 (PG 91:1189C–1193C). In Maximus's vision, God will graciously
raise his creatures from being, to well-being, and beyond this to "eternal well-being"
as he sometimes says (cf *Amb.* 7, PG 91:1073C; *Ad Thal.* 60, CCSG 22:79, 117–120). On
the broader philosophical parameters of Maximus's cosmology, see Torstein Tollefsen, *The Christocentric Cosmology of St. Maximus the Confessor: A Study of His Metaphysical Principles,* Acta Humaniora 72 (Oslo: Unipub Forlag, 2000).

[3]Envisioning the activity of the cosmos as a whole, Maximus presupposes here,
as elsewhere, that the overcoming of "intentional divergence" (γνωμικὴ διάφορα),
the self-centered deliberative movement of creatures, will be requisite to the restoration of all things to the Creator.

[4]Such is a most important reminder that Maximus projects not only the deification of human beings but of the universe as a whole: a cosmic transfiguration. Cf
Amb. 41 (PG 91:1308D–1313B), where, commenting on Gregory Nazianzen's celebrated phrase that the "natures are innovated" in the incarnation, Maximus explains
in depth how Christ the Logos harmonizes and transfigures the whole creation by
uniting in himself the *logoi* of universals and particulars. For an English translation
of *Amb.* 41, see Louth, *Maximus the Confessor,* pp. 155–62.

[5]This kind of trinitarian amplification is found in Maximus's predecessor Gregory Nazianzen (*Or. theol.* 2.1, SC 250:100), and has parallels elsewhere in the

through all and in all things (Eph 4:6), contemplated as the whole reality proportionately in each individual creature as it is deemed worthy by grace, and in the universe altogether, just as the soul naturally indwells both the whole of the body and each individual part without diminishing itself.

Confessor's own writings, most notably *Ad Thal.* 60 (CCSG 22:79, 94–105), and his *Commentary on the Lord's Prayer* (CCSG 23:30, 91–96). On these kinds of trinitarian enhancements, see Felix Heinzer, "L'explication trinitaire de l'économie chez Maxime le Confesseur," in *Maximus Confessor: Actes du symposium sur Maxime le Confesseur, Fribourg, 2–5 septembre 1980*, ed. Felix Heinzer and Christoph Schönborn, Paradosis 27 (Fribourg: Éditions Universitaires, 1982), pp. 160–72.

On the Grace of Holy Baptism

(CCSG 7:69–71)

Q. [69] If, as St John says, *he who is born of God does not sin, because his seed dwells in God, and he cannot sin* (1 Jn 3:9), and yet he who is born of water and Spirit is himself born of God (cf Jn 3:5–6), then how are we who are born of God through baptism still able to sin?

R. The manner of birth from God within us is two-fold: the one bestows the grace of adoption, which is entirely present in potency (δυνάμει) in those who are born of God; the other introduces, wholly by active exertion (κατ᾽ ἐνέργειαν), that grace which deliberately (γνωμικῶς) reorients the entire free choice of the one being born of God toward the God who gives birth.[1] The first bears the grace, present in potency, through faith alone; but the second, beyond faith, also engenders in the knower the sublimely divine likeness of the One known, that likeness being effected precisely through knowledge. Therefore the first manner of birth is observed in some because their will (γνώμη), not yet fully detached from its propensity to the flesh, has yet to be wholly endowed with the Spirit by participation in the divine mysteries that are made known through active endeavor. The inclination to sin does not disappear as long as they will it. For the Spirit does not give birth to an unwilling will (γνώμη), but converts

---

[1] Maximus's "realized eschatology" (see *Ad Thalassium* 22 below) informs his whole understanding of the "potentiality" and "actuality" of the grace of deification. The full fruition of the grace of adoption is already present, at least potentially, in the believer, before it becomes actually operative in the spiritual life.

the willing will toward deification.[2] Whoever has participated in this deification through cognizant experience[3] is incapable of reverting from right discernment in truth, once he has achieved this in action, to something else besides, which only pretends to be that same discernment. It is like the eye which, once it has looked upon the sun, cannot mistake it for the moon or any of the other stars in the heavens. With those undergoing the (second mode of) birth, the Holy Spirit takes the whole of their free choice and translates it completely from earth to heaven, and, through the true knowledge acquired by exertion, transfigures the mind with the blessed light-rays of our God and Father, such that the mind is deemed another "god," insofar as in its habitude it experiences, [71] by grace, that which God himself does not experience but "is" in his very essence. With those undergoing this second mode of baptism, their free choice clearly becomes sinless in virtue and knowledge, as they are unable to negate what they have actively discerned through experience. So even if we have the Spirit of adoption, who is himself the Seed for enduing those begotten (through baptism) with the likeness of the Sower, but do not present him with a will cleansed of any inclination or disposition to something else, we therefore, even after being born of water and Spirit (Jn 3:5), willingly sin. But were we to prepare our will with knowledge to receive the operation of these agents—water and Spirit, I mean—then the mystical water would, through our practical life, cleanse our conscience, and the life-giving Spirit would bring about unchanging perfection of the good in us through knowledge acquired in experience. Precisely for that reason he leaves, to each of us who are still able to sin, the sheer desire to surrender our whole selves willingly to the Spirit.

[2]This discussion in *Ad Thalassium* 6 provides another remarkable instance, from his earlier writings, of Maximus's positive appraisal of the role of "gnomic" will in the spiritual life, and even in the transition to deification.

[3]On Maximus's sophisticated language of religious "experience" (πεῖρα) and this allusion in particular, see Pierre Miquel, "Πεῖρα: Contribution à l'étude du vocabulaire de l'expérience religieuse dans l'oeuvre de Maxime le Confesseur," *Studia Patristica* 7, Texte und Untersuchungen 92 (Berlin: Akademie-Verlag, 1966), pp. 355–61 (especially p. 358).

AD THALASSIUM 17

On Spiritual Progress in Virtue

(CCSG 7:111–115)

Q. [111] If God sent Moses off to Egypt, then why did the angel of God seek to kill him who had been sent by God? Indeed the angel would have killed him, had Moses's anxious wife not circumcised their young son and thereby curbed the angel's wrath (cf Ex 4:19–26). And if the circumcision of the little boy was necessary, why did God not kindly enjoin Moses to circumcise the boy before he ever sent him on his way? Why indeed, if Moses had mistakenly failed to circumcise his son, did the good angel not kindly warn him, as he was being sent off, to perform such a service on his son?

R. Whoever intelligently examines the enigmas of the Scriptures with a fear of God and for the sake of the divine glory alone, and removes the letter as though it were a curtain around the spirit, *shall discover everything face to face*, as the wise proverb says (Prov 8:9). No impediment will be found to the perfect motion of the mind toward divine things. Therefore we shall let stand the literal meaning that has already been corporeally fulfilled in Moses's time and consider, with spiritual eyes, the power of the literal meaning in the Spirit, since this power is constantly being realized and abounding into its fullness.

   The desert (Ex 3:1) from which Moses was sent to Egypt to lead out the sons of Israel represents either human nature, or this world, or that habitude (of the soul) which has been ridded of the passions. The mind who, subsisting in that habitude and dwelling in this world, is instructed in true knowledge through the contemplation of created beings, receives a hidden and mystical commission from God invisibly to lead out of the *Egypt* of the heart—that is, from [the realm of] flesh and sense—divine thoughts of created beings, in the manner of the Israelites. For such thoughts are uselessly spent on clay, that is, on the passions of the flesh. Yet [113] the mind who remains faithful in this divine ministry—having gnostic wisdom joined with him like a companion, and having the noble demeanor and reflection that arise therewith—invariably travels in a holy way of life the road of the virtues, a road that in no way admits of any stalling on the part of those who walk in it. On the contrary, this mind runs the ever-moving, swift race of the soul toward *the goal of the upward call* (Phil 3:14). For the immobility of virtue is the beginning of vice.[1] When the mind, in subjection to passion, is vexed by material obstacles intruding from either side in its way, it profanes and renders uncircumcised the pure and wholly circumcised conduct and reflection that arise from godly living.

And so one spiritually envisions the reproving word (of God) forthwith as an *angel* threatening death in the conscience, and testifying that the reason for this threat is immobility in virtue, such as also causes the uncircumcision of mental reflection. The wisdom that dwells with the mind wins over its reflection, and, in the manner of Zipporah, uses the *small stone* (Ex 4:25) of the word of faith

    [1]Maximus is clearly deferring here to Gregory of Nyssa's portrait of Moses as a model of "perpetual striving" (ἐπέκτασις) toward God, based on Paul's image of the runner's striving (ἐπεκτεινόμενος) in Phil 3:14. Maximus simply paraphrases Gregory's own statement that "Just as the end of life is the beginning of death, so also stopping in the race of virtue marks the beginning of evil" (*Vita Moysis*, Book 1, GNO 7, pt. 1, 3.21–23, trans. Everett Ferguson and Abraham Malherbe, *Gregory of Nyssa: The Life of Moses*, Classics of Western Spirituality [Ramsay, N.J.: Paulist Press, 1978], p. 30). Gregory had expanded at length on the sublime paradox that true repose, the soul's spiritual sabbath, is achieved only through eternal movement in the pursuit of virtue. On Maximus's dependence on Gregory here, see Blowers, "Maximus the Confessor, Gregory of Nyssa, and the Concept of 'Perpetual Progress,' " pp. 155–6.

to circumcise the material illusion that arises in the little boy—that is, in mental reflection—and to eliminate any thought of sensual life. For Zipporah said, *the blood of the boy's circumcision has been instituted* (Ex 4:25), which is to say that the passion-laden life and illusion and motion (of the soul) abate once the defiled reflection (of the mind) has been purified with the wisdom of faith. Therewith the word (of God), which like an angel smites the errant mind through the conscience and frustrates every emerging thought save that which properly befits it, suspends its purification. For the way of the virtues is in truth filled with many holy angels who can effect every specific virtue. I am really speaking of the principles and modes of the virtues. They are the "angels" who cooperate with us in pursuing what is good and who elicit such principles (of virtue) within us.

Therefore the word of Holy Scripture remains good and noble, always offering spiritual truth in place of the literal for those who lay hold of its saving meaning with the eyes of the soul. The scriptural word contains nothing slanderous of God or his holy [115] angels. For according to the spiritual sense of this text, when God sent Moses on his way he did not have an uncircumcised son, or rather thought, otherwise God would have commissioned him in the first place to circumcise his son. Moreover, the divine angel was not being harsh when he warned Moses of the death that would befall him by being errantly immobile in the way of the virtues. On the (moral) racecourse, weakness in performing the virtues can result in just such a death.

Those of you who rely more precisely on the literal meaning of the story will notice that the angel who went to meet Moses and threaten him with death for the passion that secretly arose in his mind, did so not at the beginning or middle or end of the road, but in the inn. You will notice that had Moses not desisted from his course and stopped his journey, he would not have been accused, not been blamed for his boy's being uncircumcised.[2]

[2]This is one of the rare places in the *Ad Thalassium* where Maximus holds up the value of the literal interpretation of an Old Testament narrative, though clearly he

If indeed we are walking in the way of the divine commandments, we should entreat God not to suspend the death that follows
from our every transgression, and to send us the "angel" of his illu-
mining word within our conscience, so that when we perceive it, we
will learn by enlightened wisdom to circumcise, like the foreskin, the
impurity of the passions that secretly arises in us in the moral race
course of life.

sees, even at this level, a harmony with the higher spiritual sense he has already set
forth, for he surmises the likelihood that a certain deviant "passion" had arisen in
Moses's mind and inhibited his journey. See the analysis of Maximus's exegesis in
Ad Thal. 17 in Blowers, *Exegesis and Spiritual Pedagogy in Maximus the Confessor*,
pp. 63–5.

On Christ's Conquest of the Human Passions

(CCSG 7:127–133)

Q. [127] What is the meaning of the scripture, *He put off the powers and principalities*, and so on (Col 2:15)? And how indeed had he "put them on" at all when he was begotten without sin?[1]

R. The divine Logos assumed our human nature without altering his divinity, and became perfect man in every way like us save without sin (cf Heb 4:15). He appeared like the first man Adam in the manner both of his creaturely origin (γένεσις) and his birth (γέννησις).[2] The first man received his existence from God and came into being at the very origin of his existence,[3] and was free from corruption and sin—for God did not create either of these. When, however, he

---

[1]Thalassius appears puzzled by Paul's language of Christ "putting off" (ἀπεκδυσάμενος) the powers and principalities as though it necessarily implies an investing or "putting on" (ἐνδυσάμενος) of them beforehand.

[2]A scholium, or note, appended to Maximus's response here summarizes succinctly his distinction between γένεσις and γέννησις: "[Maximus] calls the original formation of man by God his origin (γένεσις), and the succession of the race by mutual (sexual) relations, which was subsequently imposed by divine judgment as a consequence of man's transgression, his procreation (γέννησις)." Maximus will expand on this distinction here in *Ad Thal.* 21, but for the same distinction see also *Amb.* 42 (PG 91:1316C–D).

[3]Maximus doubtless adds this as an anti-Origenist caveat: there was no spiritual preexistence of the first human being, rather, he came into physical existence at a specific point in time and space according to God's creative intention. Moreover, there

sinned by breaking God's commandment, he was condemned to
birth based on sexual passion and sin. Sin henceforth constrained
his true natural origin within the liability to passions that had accompanied the first sin, as though placing it under a law. Accordingly, there is no human being who is sinless, since everyone is
naturally subject to the law of sexual procreation that was introduced after man's true creaturely origin in consequence of his sin.

Since, therefore, sin came about on account of the transgression,
and the liability to passions connected with sexual procreation entered human nature on account of sin, and since, through sin, the
original transgression continued unabatedly to flourish right along
with this passibility of childbirth, there was no hope of liberation,
for human nature was deliberately[4] and indissolubly bound by the
chain of evil. The more human nature sought to preserve itself
through sexual procreation, the more tightly it bound itself to the
law of sin, reactivating the transgression connected with the liability
to passions. Because of its physical condition, human nature suffered the increase of sin within this very liability to passions, and it
retained the energies of all opposing forces, principalities, and powers—energies which, in view of the universal sin operative in human
passibility, used the unnatural passions to hide under the guise of
natural passions. Wherefore every wicked power is at work, amid
human nature's liability to passions, [129] driving the deliberative
will (γνώμη) with the natural passions into the corruption of unnatural passions.

Thus, in his love of humanity, the only-begotten Son and Logos
of God became perfect man, with a view to redeeming human

---

was no "second" bodily creation after the fall, but only a subjection to the multiple
passions (see *Ad Thal.* 1 translated above).

[4]Crucial to Maximus's anthropology is the conviction that sin has continued to
perpetuate itself in the human race not by "natural volition" (φυσικὴ θέλημα) but by
the vacillating, deliberating "gnomic" will (γνώμη). Despite its ambiguous ontological status, the gnomic will nonetheless has enormous existential ramifications for the
reorientation and redemption of human volition, for which reason Maximus questioned whether there was a gnomic will operative in Christ himself.

nature from this helplessness in evil. Taking on the original condition of Adam as he was in the very beginning (γένεσις), he was sinless but not incorruptible, and he assumed, from the procreative
process (γέννησις) introduced into human nature as a consequence
of sin, only the liability to passions, not the sin itself.[5] Since, then,
through the liability to passions that resulted from Adam's sin, the
evil powers, as I already said, have hidden their activities clandes-
tinely under the law of human nature in its current circumstance,[6]
it merely follows that these wicked powers—seeing in God our Savior the same natural liability to passions as in Adam, since he was in
the flesh, and thinking that he was necessarily and circumstantially
a mere man, that the Lord himself had to submit to the law of nature,
that he acted by deliberation rather than true volition—assailed
him. These evil powers hoped to use natural passibility to induce
even the Lord himself to fantasize unnatural passion and to do what
suited them. They tried to do this to him who, in his first experience
of temptation by pleasure, subjected himself to being deluded by
these evil powers' deceits, only to *put off* those powers by eliminat-
ing them from human nature, remaining unapproachable and
untouchable for them. Clearly he won the victory over them for our
sake, not for his own; and it was for us that he became a man and, in
his goodness, inaugurated a complete restoration. For he himself did
not need the experience, since he is God and Sovereign and by
nature free from all passion. He submitted to it so that, by experiencing our temptations, he might provoke the evil power and thwart
its attack, putting to death the very power that expected to seduce
him just as it had Adam in the beginning.

[5]Elsewhere Maximus explicitly describes the virginal conception and birth of
Christ (the New Adam) as the very means by which he inaugurates the new *tropos* of
human existence: cf *Amb.* 31 (PG 91:1273D–1276D); ibid. 42 (1313C–D). Indeed, precisely in his becoming incarnate through the virginal birth he overcomes the division
between male and female altogether (*Amb.* 41, PG 91:1309A–B).

[6]τῷ περιστατικῷ νόμῳ τῆς φύσεως. Maximus speaks of the "law" of human
nature as operating, now, after the fall, in a contingent or circumstantial (περιστα-
τικός) mode—i.e., within the constraints of the liability so passions, yet still under
the broader redemptive and providential economy of God.

This, then, is how, in his initial experience of temptation, he *put off the principalities and powers*, removing them from human nature and (healing the liability) to hedonistic passions, and in himself *cancelled the bond* (Col 2:14) of Adam's deliberate acquiescence in those hedonistic passions. For it is by this bond that man's will (γνώμη) inclines toward wicked pleasure against his own best interest, and that man declares, [131] in the very silence of his works, his enslavement, being unable, in his fear of death, to free himself from his slavery to pleasure.

Then, after having overcome and frustrated the forces of evil, the *principalities and powers*, through his first experience of being tempted with pleasure, the Lord allowed them to attack him a second time and to provoke him, through pain and toil, with the further experience of temptation so that, by completely depleting them, within himself, of the deadly poison of their wickedness, he might utterly consume it, as though in a [refiner's] fire. For he *put off the principalities and powers* at the moment of his death on the cross, when he remained impervious to his sufferings and, what is more, manifested the (natural human) fear of death, thereby driving from our nature the passion associated with pain.[7] Man's will, out of cowardice, tends away from suffering, and man, against his own will, remains utterly dominated by the fear of death, and, in his desire to live, clings to his slavery to pleasure.

[7]The issue of Jesus's natural human fear of death is one which Maximus raises early in his writing, in the *Commentary on the Lord's Prayer* (CCSG 23:34, 135–35, 142), where he affirms a "gnomic," or deliberative, will in Jesus but urges that in the face of death, Jesus did not waver but thoroughly stabilized his γνώμη. Yet the issue became acute later on in the heat of the Monothelite controversy, where Maximus ultimately denied a gnomic will in Christ, and spelled out more fully the character of Jesus's fear of death in his christological *Opuscula* on the Agony of Christ in Gethsemane (see *Opusc.* 6, trans. below, pp. 173–6 and also note 4) and in his *Disputation with Pyrrhus*. In the *Disputation* (PG 91:297B), he indicates that Christ blamelessly "used" fear for our sake, in effect pioneering a new and edifying mode of that fear as part of the conforming of human volition to the divine will. On this point, see also Pierre Piret, *Le Christ et la Trinité*, pp. 281–2; and Paul Blowers, "The Passion of Jesus Christ in Maximus the Confessor: A Reconsideration," especially pp. 368–9, 376.

So the Lord *put off the principalities and powers* at the time of his first experience of temptation in the desert, thereby healing the whole of human nature of the passion connected with pleasure. Yet he despoiled them again at the time of his death, in that he likewise eliminated from our human nature the passion connected with pain. In his love of humanity, he accomplished this restoration for us as though he were himself liable; and what is more, in his goodness, he reckoned to us the glory of what he had restored. So too, since he assumed our nature's liability to passions, albeit without sin (cf Heb 4:10), thereby inciting every evil power and destructive force to go into action, he despoiled them at the moment of his death, right when they came after him to search him out. He *triumphed* (Col 2:15) over them and made a spectacle of them in his cross, at the departure of his soul, when the evil powers could find nothing at all [culpable] in the passibility proper to his human nature. For they certainly expected to find something utterly human in him, in view of his natural carnal liability to passions. It seems that in his proper power and, as it were, by a certain "first fruits" of his holy and humanly begotten flesh, he completely freed our human nature [133] from the evil which had insinuated itself therein through the liability to passions. For he subjugated—to this very same natural passibility—the evil tyranny which had once ruled within it (within that passibility, I mean).

It would be possible to interpret this text differently, in a more mystical and sublime sense. As you know, however, we must not commit the ineffable truths of the divine teachings of Scripture to writing. Let us rest content with what has been said, which should assuage our curiosity about this text. With God's help, and as long as it will be found worthy in your eyes, we shall still inquire, with a zeal to learn, into the apostolic thinking on this.

On Jesus Christ and the
End of the Ages

(ccsg 7:137–143)

Q. [137] If *in the coming ages* God *will show his riches* (Eph 2:7), how is it that *the end of the ages has* [already] *come upon us* (1 Cor 10:11)?

R. He who, by the sheer inclination of his will, established the beginning of all creation, seen and unseen, before all the ages and before that beginning of created beings, had an ineffably good plan for those creatures. The plan was for him to mingle, without change on his part, with human nature by true hypostatic union, to unite human nature to himself while remaining immutable, so that he might become a man, as he alone knew how, and so that he might deify humanity in union with himself. Also, according to this plan, it is clear that God wisely divided "the ages" (αἰῶνες) between those intended for God to become human, and those intended for humanity to become divine.

Thus *the end* of those ages predetermined for God to become human has already *come upon us*, since God's purpose was fulfilled in the very events of his incarnation. The divine Apostle, having fully examined this fact [. . .],[1] and observing that the end of the ages intended for God's becoming human had already arrived through

---

[1]There is a small lacuna in the Greek text at this point.

the very incarnation of the divine Logos, said that *the end of the ages has come upon us* (1 Cor 10:11). Yet by "ages" he meant not ages as we normally conceive them, but clearly the ages intended to bring about the mystery of his embodiment, which have already come to term according to God's purpose.

Since, therefore, the ages predetermined in God's purpose for the realization of his becoming human have reached their end for us, and God has undertaken and in fact achieved his own perfect incarnation, the other "ages"—those which are to come about for the realization of the mystical and ineffable deification of humanity—must follow henceforth. In these new ages God [139] *will show the immeasurable riches of his goodness to us* (Eph 2:7), having completely realized this deification in those who are worthy. For if he has brought to completion his mystical work of becoming human, having become like us in every way save without sin (cf Heb 4:15), and even descended into the lower regions of the earth where the tyranny of sin compelled humanity, then God will also completely fulfill the goal of his mystical work of deifying humanity in every respect, of course, short of an identity of essence with God; and he will assimilate humanity to himself and elevate us to a position above all the heavens. It is to this exalted position that the natural magnitude of God's grace summons lowly humanity, out of a goodness that is infinite. The great Apostle is mystically teaching us about this when he says that *in the ages to come the immeasurable riches of his goodness will be shown to us* (Eph 2:7).

We too should therefore divide the "ages" conceptually, and distinguish between those intended for the mystery of the divine incarnation and those intended for the grace of human deification, and we shall discover that the former have already reached their proper end while the latter have not yet arrived. In short, the former have to do with God's descent to human beings, while the latter have to do with humanity's ascent to God. By interpreting the texts thus, we do not falter in the obscurity of the divine words of Scripture, nor assume that the divine Apostle had lapsed into this same mistake.

Or rather, since our Lord Jesus Christ is the beginning (ἀρχή), middle (μεσότης), and end (τέλος) of all the ages,[2] past and future, [it would be fair to say that] the *end of the ages*—specifically that end which will actually come about by grace for the deification of those who are worthy—*has come upon us* in potency through faith.[3]

Or again, since there is one principle of activity and another [141] of passivity, [we could say that] the divine Apostle has mystically and wisely distinguished the active principle from the passive principle respectively in the past and future "ages." Accordingly, the ages of the flesh, in which we now live (for Scripture also knows the ages of time, as when it says that man *toiled in this age and shall live until its end* [Ps 48:10]) are characterized by activity, while the future ages in the Spirit, which are to follow the present life, are characterized by the transformation of humanity in passivity. Existing here and now, we arrive at the *end of the ages* as active agents and reach the end of the exertion of our power and activity. But in the ages to come we shall undergo by grace the transformation unto deification and no longer be active but passive; and for this reason we shall not cease from being deified. At that point our passion will be supernatural, and there will be no principle restrictive of the divine activity in infinitely deifying those who are passive to it. For we are active agents insofar as we have operative, by nature, a rational faculty for performing the virtues, and also a spiritual faculty, unlimited in its potential, capable of receiving all knowledge, capable of transcending the nature of all created beings and known things and even of leaving the "ages" of time behind it. But when in the future we are rendered passive (in deification), and have fully transcended the principles of beings created out of nothing, we will unwittingly enter into the true Cause of existent beings and terminate our proper

---

[2]Cf *Ad Thalassium* 19 (CCSG 7:119, 7–30).

[3]For this "realized" eschatology as expressed in Maximus's baptismal theology, see above, *Ad Thalassium* 6 (translated above), where he suggests that the grace of adoption (and so too deification) is already fully present "in potency" through faith before it is actualized through the knowledge acquired in spiritual experience.

faculties along with everything in our nature that has reached completion. We shall become that which in no way results from our natural ability, since our human nature has no faculty for grasping what transcends nature. For nothing created is by its nature capable of inducing deification, since it is incapable of comprehending God. Intrinsically it is only by the grace of God that deification is bestowed proportionately on created beings. Grace alone illuminates human nature with supernatural light, and, by the superiority of its glory, elevates our nature above its proper limits in excess of glory.[4]

So it does not seem, then, that *the end of the ages has come upon us* (1 Cor 10:11) since we have not yet received, by the grace that is in Christ, [143] the gift of benefits that transcend time and nature. Meanwhile, the modes of the virtues and the principles of those things that can be known by nature have been established as types and foreshadowings of those future benefits. It is through these modes and principles that God, who is ever willing to become human, does so in those who are worthy. And therefore whoever, by the exercise of wisdom, enables God to become incarnate within him or her and, in fulfillment of this mystery, undergoes deification by grace, is truly blessed, because that deification has no end. For he who bestows his grace on those who are worthy of it is himself infinite in essence, and has the infinite and utterly limitless power to deify humanity. Indeed, this divine power is not yet finished with those beings created by it; rather, it is forever sustaining those—like us human beings—who have received their existence from it. Without it they could not exist. This is why the text speaks of the *riches of his goodness* (Eph 2:7), since God's resplendent plan for our transformation unto deification never ceases in its goodness toward us.

<hr>

[4]Notably, Maximus has tendered four different possible interpretations of Thalassius's query, each of them valid. On these explanations, see Paul M. Blowers, "Realized Eschatology in Maximus the Confessor, *Ad Thalassium* 22," *Studia Patristica* 32, ed. Elizabeth Livingstone (Leuven: Peeters Press, 1997), pp. 258–63.

On Jesus Christ, the New Adam Who "Became Sin"

(CCSG 7:285–289)

Q. [285] How is it that we are said to commit sin and know it (cf 1 Jn 1:8), while the Lord became sin but did not know it? How is it not more serious to become sin and not know it, than to commit sin and know it? For the Scripture says, *For our sake God made him become sin who knew no sin* (2 Cor 5:21).

R. Having originally been corrupted from its natural design, Adam's free choice (προαίρεσις) corrupted along with it our human nature, which forfeited the grace of impassibility (ἀπάθεια). Thus came sin into existence. The first sin, culpable indeed, was the fall of free choice from good into evil; the second, following upon the first, was the innocent transformation of human nature from incorruption into corruption. For our forefather Adam committed two "sins" by his transgression of God's commandment: the first "sin" was culpable, when his free choice willfully rejected the good; but the second "sin," occasioned by the first, was innocent, since human nature unwillingly put off its incorruption. Therefore our Lord and God, rectifying this reciprocal corruption and alteration of our human nature by taking on the whole of our nature, even had in his assumed nature the liability to passions which, in his own exercise of free choice, he adorned with incorruptibility. And it is by virtue of his assumption of this natural passibility that he *became sin for our sake*, though he did not *know* any deliberate sin (γνωμικὴ ἁμαρτία) because of the immutability of his free choice.[1] Because his free choice was incorruptible, he rectified our nature's liability to passions and turned the end of our nature's passibility—which is death—into the beginning of our natural transformation to incorruption. In turn, just as through one man, who turned voluntarily from the good, the human nature was changed from incorruption to corruption to the detriment of all humanity, so too through one man, Jesus Christ, who did not voluntarily turn from the good, [287] human nature underwent a restoration from corruption to incorruption for the benefit of all humanity.[2]

Therefore the Lord did not *know* "my sin" (ἡ ἐμὴ ἁμαρτία), that is, the mutability of my free choice. Neither did he assume nor *become* my sin. Rather, he *became* the "sin that I caused" (ἡ δι᾽ ἐμὲ ἁμαρτία); in other words, he assumed the corruption of human nature that was a consequence of the mutability of my free choice. For our sake he became a human being naturally liable to passions, and used the "sin" that I caused to destroy the "sin" that I commit. Just as in Adam, with his own act of freely choosing evil, the common glory of human nature, incorruption, was robbed—since God judged that it was not right for humanity, having abused free choice, to have an immortal nature—so too in Christ, with his own act of

[1]Just as in another of his early works, the *Commentary on the Lord's Prayer* (CCSG 23:34, 135–35, 142), Maximus had openly avowed the presence of "gnomic" will in Christ, here in *Ad Thalassium* 42 he affirms the presence of "free choice" (προαίρεσις) in Christ as well. Later, in the heat of the Monothelite controversy, he would retract that assertion. He does so in *Opusculum* 1, (PG 91:29D–32A), written ca. 645, where he refers back to *Ad Thalassium* 42 and explains that to affirm "free choice" (προαίρεσις) in Christ would be to introduce an ordinary process of appetency in his already-deified human will (θέλησις). At this point, "free choice" could all too easily be associated with γνώμη, which Maximus had at last narrowly defined as that "deliberative" sort of volition which entailed hesitancy toward the good, and which could not, then, be operative in Christ.

[2]Cf Paul's Adam/Christ analogy in Rom 5:12–19; 1 Cor 15:21–22.

freely choosing the good, the common scourge of our whole nature, corruption, was taken away. At the resurrection of Christ, human nature was transformed into incorruption because his free choice was immutable. For God judged that it was right for man, when he did not subvert his free choice, once again to recover an immortal nature. By "man" here I mean the incarnate Logos in virtue of the fact that he united to himself, hypostatically, the flesh animated by a rational soul. For if the deviance[3] of free choice introduced passibility, corruptibility, and mortality in Adam's nature, it only followed that in Christ, the immutability of free choice, realized through his resurrection, introduced natural impassibility, incorruptibility, and immortality.

Hence the mutation of human nature over to passibility, corruption, and death is the condemnation of Adam's deliberate sin. Man was not created by God in the beginning with such a corrupted nature; rather, man invented and *knew* it since he created deliberate sin through his disobedience. And clearly condemnation by death is the result of such sin. Yet the Lord took on this very condemnation of my deliberate sin, that is to say, the passibility, corruptibility, and mortality of our nature. [289] He *became the "sin" that I caused*, in terms of the passibility, corruptibility, and mortality, and he submitted voluntarily to the condemnation owed me in my nature, even though he himself was blameless in his freedom of choice, in order to condemn both my deliberate "sin" and the "sin" that befell my nature. Accordingly he has driven sin, passion, corruption, and death from human nature, and the economy of Christ's philanthropy on my behalf has become for me, one fallen through disobedience, a new mystery. For the sake of my salvation, Christ, through

[3]The notion of the mutability (τροπή), or, understood pejoratively, the "deviance" of human free choice, well known from the anthropology of Gregory of Nyssa, was exploited by Maximus as well. See, in particular, *Ep.* 6 (PG 91:432A–B); also Paul Blowers, "Maximus the Confessor, Gregory of Nyssa, and the Concept of 'Perpetual Progress,'" *Vigiliae Christianae* 46 (1992): 156–7. On the antecedent development of this theme in Gregory, see Jean Daniélou, *L'être et le temps chez Grégoire de Nysse* (Leiden: E. J. Brill, 1970), pp. 95–115.

his own death, voluntarily made my condemnation his own, thereby granting me restoration to immortality.

In many ways, I think, it has been shown in this brief discussion both how the Lord *became sin* but did not *know* it, and how humanity did not become sin but did commit and know sin—both the deliberate "sin" which man committed first, and the subsequent natural "sin" to which the Lord submitted himself on humanity's account, even when he was completely free of the first kind of sin. So according to the intended purpose (σκοπός) of the text as we have rendered it here,[4] and respecting the proper conceptual distinction between the two meanings of "sin," it is by no means better to commit and to know sin than to *become* sin. For the former "sin" incurs separation from God, since free choice voluntarily rejects divine things; but the latter "sin" may very well hinder evil, since it does not allow that wickedness of free choice that is based on the infirmity of nature to advance into concrete action.

[4]Maximus presupposes the Alexandrian hermeneutical principle of the ultimate "intention" (σκοπός) of scriptural texts, their pointing beyond themselves to a higher spiritual and eschatological purpose. The principle is found abundantly in Origen, Gregory of Nyssa, and other Greek patristic exegetes prior to Maximus.

On the Cosmic Mystery of Jesus Christ

(CCSG 22:73–81)

Q. [73] ... *of Christ, as of a pure and spotless lamb, who was foreknown before the foundation of the world, yet manifested at the end of time for our sake* (1 Pet 1:20). By whom was Christ foreknown?

R. The scriptural text calls the mystery of Christ "Christ." The great Apostle clearly testifies to this when he speaks of *the mystery hidden from the ages, having now been manifested* (Col 1:26). He is of course referring to Christ the whole mystery of Christ, which is, manifestly, the ineffable and incomprehensible hypostatic union between Christ's divinity and humanity. This union draws his humanity into perfect identity, in every way, with his divinity, through the principle of person (ὑπόστασις); it is a union that realizes one person composite of both natures,[1] inasmuch as it in no way diminishes the essential difference between those natures. And so, to repeat, there is one hypostasis realized from the two natures and the difference

---

[1] The terminology and conceptualization of the "composite" (σύνθετος) character of the union of divine and human natures in Christ had a long and tortured history in the early christological controversies. The battle to understand the coming together of the natures in terms of *compositeness* but not *confusion* had already been won by Maximus's time, and Maximus rests content that the Chalcedonian Definition of the hypostasis of Christ has once for all secured the principle of a union without violation of the two distinct natures.

between the natures remains immutable. In view of this difference, moreover, the natures remain undiminished, and the quantity of each of the united natures is preserved, even after the union. For, whereas by the union no change or alteration at all was suffered by either of the united natures, the essential principle of each of the united natures endured without being compromised. Indeed that essential principle remained inviolate even after the union, as the divine and human natures retained their integrity in every respect. Neither of the natures was denied anything at all because of the union.

For it was fitting for the Creator of the universe, who by the economy of his incarnation became what by nature he was not, to preserve without change both what he himself was by nature and what he became in his incarnation. [75] For naturally we must not consider any change at all in God, nor conceive any movement in him. Being changed properly pertains to movable creatures.[2] This is the great and hidden mystery, at once the blessed end for which all things are ordained. It is the divine purpose conceived before the beginning of created beings. In defining it we would say that this mystery is the preconceived goal for which everything exists, but which itself exists on account of nothing.[3] With a clear view to this end, God created the essences of created beings, and such is, properly speaking, the terminus of his providence and of the things under his providential care. Inasmuch as it leads to God, it is the recapitulation of the things he has created.[4] It is the mystery which circumscribes all the ages, and which reveals the grand plan of God

[2]The cosmological and soteriological implications of Maximus's doctrine of the immobility of God and the mobility of created beings in relation to God are developed most fully in *Amb.* 7 (PG 91:1069A–1077B), translated above.

[3]Since God is himself the final goal (τέλος) of all creation, and depends for his existence on nothing outside of himself.

[4]Maximus here reintroduces, in his own post-Chalcedonian context, the Pauline theme of the incarnation of Jesus Christ as a summation, or recapitulation (ἀνακε-φαλαίωσις), of God's creative purposes—a theme already substantially developed by Maximus's distant predecessor in the second century, Irenaeus of Lyons, in his polemic against Gnostic cosmologies.

(cf Eph 1:10–11), a super-infinite plan infinitely preexisting the ages.[5] The Logos, by essence God, became a messenger of this plan (cf Isa 9:5, LXX) when he became a man and, if I may rightly say so, established himself as the innermost depth of the Father's goodness while also displaying in himself the very goal for which his creatures manifestly received the beginning of their existence.[6]

Because of Christ—or rather, the whole mystery of Christ—all the ages of time and the beings within those ages have received their beginning and end in Christ. For the union between a limit of the ages and limitlessness, between measure and immeasurability, between finitude and infinity, between Creator and creation, between rest and motion, was conceived before the ages. This union has been manifested in Christ at the end of time, and in itself brings God's foreknowledge to fulfillment, in order that naturally mobile creatures might secure themselves around God's total and essential immobility, desisting altogether from their movement toward themselves and toward each other.[7] The union has been manifested so that they might also acquire, by experience, an active knowledge of him [77] in whom they were made worthy to find their stability

[5]Cf *Amb.* 7 (PG 91:1096B–1097D); ibid. 41 (1308D–1309A).

[6]See *Ad Thalassium* 22 (CCSG 7:139, 60–64), where Maximus speaks of Christ himself as the "beginning" (ἀρχή), "middle" (μεσότης) and "end" (τέλος) of all creation; cf also *Ad Thal.* 19 (CCSG 7:119, 7–30).

[7]Maximus here refers to the absolute stability (στάσις) which is the goal (τέλος) of all creaturely movement, a notion which he elsewhere (*Amb.* 7 PG 91:1073B) directed against the Origenist cosmology in which true *stasis* is that original, primordial spiritual unity, prior to the fall of intellectual beings, to which all creatures are called, amid the instability of history, in a final and complete restoration (ἀποκατάστασις), literally, the "recovery of *stasis.*" For Maximus, however, the final end of creaturely movement is an unprecedented new rest in the Divine at the end of the cosmic story, that stability "around the Divine" (περὶ τὸ θεῖον, *Ep.* 6, PG 91:432B) or around God's immobility, which brings everything to sabbatical completion. Maximus is sympathetic to Gregory of Nyssa's image of this ultimate "repose" as secured precisely in "perpetual striving" (ἐπέκτασις), an eternal purposive movement around the God whose essence remains impenetrable. On the philosophical and theological ramifications of this notion, see Paul M. Blowers, "Maximus the Confessor, Gregory of Nyssa, and the Concept of 'Perpetual Progress,'" pp. 151–71. On the ascetic implications of this notion, see *Ad Thalassium* 17 (translated above, pp. 105–8).

and to have abiding unchangeably in them the enjoyment of this knowledge.

The scriptural Word knows of two kinds of knowledge of divine things. On the one hand, there is relative knowledge, rooted only in reason and ideas, and lacking in the kind of experiential perception of what one knows through active engagement; such relative knowledge is what we use to order our affairs in our present life. On the other hand, there is that truly authentic knowledge, gained only by actual experience, apart from reason and ideas, which provides a total perception of the known object through a participation (μέθεξις) by grace. By this latter knowledge, we attain, in the future state, the supernatural deification (θέωσις) that remains unceasingly in effect. They say that the relative knowledge based on reason and ideas can motivate our desire for the participative knowledge acquired by active engagement. They say, moreover, that this active, experiential knowledge which, by participation, furnishes the direct perception of the object known, can supplant the relative knowledge based on reason and ideas.[8]

For the sages say that it is impossible for rational knowledge (λόγος) of God to coexist with the direct experience (πεῖρα) of God, or for conceptual knowledge (νόησις) of God to coexist with immediate perception (αἴσθησις) of God. By "rational knowledge of God" I mean the use of the analogy of created beings in the intellectual contemplation of God; by "perception" I mean the experience, through participation, of the supernatural goods; by "conceptual knowledge" I mean the simple and unitary knowledge of God drawn from created beings. This kind of distinction may be recognized with every other kind of knowledge as well, since the direct "experience" of a thing suspends rational knowledge of it and direct "perception" of a thing renders the "conceptual knowledge" of it useless. By "experience" (πεῖρα) I mean that knowledge, based on active engagement, which surpasses all reason. By "perception" (αἴσθησις)

[8]On this important passage in the context of Maximus's larger religious epistemology, see Pierre Miquel, "Πεῖρα: Contribution à l'étude du vocabulaire de l'expérience religieuse dans l'oeuvre de Maxime le Confesseur," pp. 359–60.

I mean that participation in the known object which manifests itself beyond all conceptualization. This may very well be what the great Apostle is secretly teaching when he says, *As for prophecies, they will pass away; as for tongues, they will cease; as for knowledge,* [79] *it will disappear* (1 Cor 13:8). Clearly he is referring here to that knowledge which is found in reason and ideas.

This mystery was known solely to the Father, the Son, and the Holy Spirit before all the ages. It was known to the Father by his approval (εὐδοκία), to the Son by his carrying it out (αὐτουργία), and to the Holy Spirit by his cooperation (συνέργεια) in it.[9] For there is one knowledge shared by the Father, the Son, and the Holy Spirit because they also share one essence and power. The Father and the Holy Spirit were not ignorant of the incarnation of the Son because the whole Father is by essence in the whole Son who himself carried out the mystery of our salvation through his incarnation. The Father himself did not become incarnate but rather approved the incarnation of the Son. Moreover, the whole Holy Spirit exists by essence in the whole Son, but he too did not become incarnate but rather cooperated in the Son's ineffable incarnation for our sake. Whether, then, one speaks of "Christ" or the "mystery of Christ," the Holy Trinity alone—Father, Son, and Holy Spirit—foreknew it. And no one should question how Christ, who is one of the Holy Trinity, was foreknown by the Trinity, when recognizing that Christ was foreknown not as God but as man. In other words, it was his incarnation for humanity's sake in the economy of salvation that was foreknown. For that which is eternal and forever transcending cause and reason could never be foreknown. Foreknowledge is of beings who have a beginning of existence because they have a cause.

[9]One may observe a similar trinitarian formula in Maximus's *Commentary on the Lord's Prayer*: "the Father gives approval, and the Spirit cooperates in the incarnation of the Son who effected it, since the Word remained in possession of his own mind and life, contained in essence by no one other than the Father and the Spirit, while hypostatically realizing out of love for man the union with the flesh" (CCSG 23:30, 91–96; trans. Berthold, *Maximus Confessor: Selected Writings*, p. 103). Cf also the formulation in *Ad Thal.* 2 (CCSG 7:51, 22–26).

Thus Christ was foreknown not as what he was in himself by nature but as what he manifested when, in the economy of salvation, he subsequently became human on our behalf. For truly he who is the Creator of the essence of created beings by nature had also to become the very Author of the deification of creatures by grace, in order that the Giver of well-being (τὸ εὖ εἶναι) might appear also as the gracious Giver of eternal well-being (τὸ ἀεὶ εὖ εἶναι). Since, therefore, no created being knows what itself or any other being absolutely is in its essence, it only follows that no created being by nature has foreknowledge of any future beings. Only God, who transcends created beings, and who knows what he himself is in essence, foreknows the existence of all his creatures [81] even before their creation. And in the future he will by grace confer on those created beings the knowledge of what they themselves and other beings are in essence, and manifest the principles of their origin which preexist uniformly in him.

Indeed, we reject the argument of some who say that Christ was *foreknown before the foundation of the world* to those to whom he was later *manifested at the end of time,* as though those beings were themselves present with the foreknown Christ before the foundation of the world, and as though the scriptural Word were running awry from the truth and suggesting that the essence of rational beings is coeternal with God.[10] For it is impossible to be completely coexistent with Christ, just as it is furthermore impossible ever to depart from him entirely, since the termination of time is fixed within Christ, as is the stability (στάσις) of mobile created beings, a stability wherein no created being will know any change at all.[11]

[10]Maximus is clearly directing his polemic here against radical Origenists, even though, as in his *Ambigua ad Joannem,* he does not identify them directly.

[11]Maximus here is simply summarizing his argument in the second and third paragraphs of this response. Not only is it ontologically impossible for a creature to enjoy preexistence or pure coexistence with Christ, it is basic to the economy of salvation and deification that the being and the movements of creatures are fixed within the physical and temporal limits which Christ, as the cosmic Logos, circumscribes.

The scriptural Word calls Christ *pure and spotless*, since in soul and body he was by nature absolutely free from the corruption of sin. For his soul did not bear the disgrace of evil, nor his body the blemish of sin.

AD THALASSIUM 61

On the Legacy of Adam's Transgression

(CCSG 22:85–105)

Q. [85] *Because the time has come for the judgment of the house of God to begin. And if we are to be judged first, what will be the end of those who disobey the gospel of God? And if the righteous man is scarcely saved, where will the impious man and the sinner appear?* (1 Pet 4:17–18). What is the meaning of the phrase *the time has come for the judgment of the house of God to begin,* and of the phrase *if the righteous man is scarcely saved?*

R. When God created human nature, he did not create sensible pleasure and pain along with it; rather, he furnished it with a certain spiritual capacity for pleasure, a pleasure whereby human beings would be able to enjoy God ineffably. But at the instant he was created,[1] the first man, by use of his senses, squandered this spiritual capacity—the natural desire of the mind for God—on sensible things. In this, his very first movement, he activated an unnatural pleasure through the medium of the senses.[2] Being, in his providence, concerned for

---

[1] ἅμα τῷ γίνεσθαι. Cf *Amb.* 42 (PG 91:1321B), trans. above, p. 85, and note 10; also *Ad Thal.* 1 (CCSG 7:47, 11), trans. above, p. 97 and note 3.

[2] In his Prologue to the *Ad Thal.* (CCSG 7:31, 240–250), Maximus explains Adam's lapse, in terms reminiscent of Gregory of Nyssa, as a fatal act of ignorance, mistaking as "God" the very thing God had commanded him to repudiate, and thus introducing

our salvation, God therefore affixed pain (ὀδύνη) alongside this
sensible pleasure (ἡδονή) as a kind of punitive faculty, whereby
the law of death was wisely implanted in our corporeal nature to curb
the foolish mind in its desire to incline unnaturally toward sensible
things.[3]

Henceforth, because irrational pleasure entered human nature,
pain entered our nature opposite this pleasure in accordance with
reason, and, through the many sufferings (παθήματα) in which and
from which death occurs, pain uproots unnatural pleasure, but does
not completely destroy it, whereby, then, the grace of the divine pleasure of the mind is naturally exalted. For every suffering (πόνος),[4]
effectively having pleasure as its primary cause, is quite naturally, in
view of its cause, a penalty exacted from all who share in human
nature. [87] Indeed, such suffering invariably accompanies unnatural pleasure in everyone for whom the law of pleasure, itself having
no prior cause, has preconditioned their birth. By that I mean that the
pleasure stemming from the original transgression was "uncaused"

a "mixed" knowledge: "The more, then, that man preoccupied himself with a knowledge based exclusively on the experience of sensible things, the more he bound himself with ignorance of God. The more he bound himself with the chain of this
ignorance, the more he cleaved to the experience of the sensual enjoyment of material objects of knowledge. The more he indulged himself in this enjoyment, the more
he aroused the desire of the self-love which it produces. The more diligently he seized
the desire of self-love, the more he invented multiple ways to sustain his pleasure,
which is the fruit and object of self-love."

    [3]On subjection to passions as a consequence of the fall, see also *Ad Thal.* 1 (above,
pp. 97–8). On the importance of the dialectic of pleasure (ἡδονή) and pain (ὀδύνη)
in Maximus's understanding of human fallenness and the economy of salvation, see
also *Ad Thal.* Prol. (CCSG 7:31, 251–33, 260), and the studies of Thunberg, *Microcosm
and Mediator*, 157–162, and Christoph Schönborn, "Plaisir et douleur dans l'analyse
de S. Maxime, d'après les *Quaestiones ad Thalassium*," in *Maximus Confessor: Actes du
Symposium sur Maxime le Confesseur, Fribourg, 2–5 septembre 1980*, ed. Felix Heinzer
and Christoph Schönborn, Paradosis 27 (Fribourg: Éditions Universitaires, 1982),
273–84.

    [4]"Suffering" (πόνος), in its usage here, can certainly include physical sufferings
(παθήματα) as such, but indicates more precisely the whole array of existential
"labors" or toils that individually manifest the universal and punitive reality of
human pain (ὀδύνη) after the fall.

(ἀναίτιον) insofar as it quite obviously did not follow upon an antecedent suffering.[5]

After the transgression pleasure naturally preconditioned the births of all human beings, and no one at all was by nature free from birth subject to the passion associated with this pleasure; rather, everyone was requited with sufferings, and subsequent death, as the natural punishment. The way to freedom was hard for all who were tyrannized by unrighteous pleasure and naturally subject to just sufferings and to the thoroughly just death accompanying them. In order for unrighteous pleasure, and the thoroughly just death which is its consequence, to be abolished (seeing as suffering humanity has been so pitiably torn asunder by them, with human beings deriving the beginning of their existence from the corruption associated with pleasure, and coming to the end of their life in the corruption of death), and in order for suffering human nature to be set right, it was necessary for an unjust and likewise uncaused suffering and death to be conceived—a death "unjust" in the sense that it by no means followed a life given to passions, and "uncaused" in the sense that it was in no way preceded by pleasure. Such a thoroughly unjust suffering and death, distinguished as intervening between unrighteous pleasure and the fully just suffering and death, would be necessary to do completely away with the unrighteous beginnings [of this legacy] in pleasure as well as the consequent just end of human nature occurring in death. In this way the human race would again be freed of pleasure and pain, and human nature would recover the good inheritance it had in the beginning, an inheritance unsullied by any indication of subjection to birth and corruption. For this reason, the Logos of God, who is fully divine by nature, became fully

[5]In this somewhat complicated statement, Maximus seems to be stressing the fact that the law of (unnatural) pleasure, while itself having no original ontological rootedness in human nature, and no "cause" (ἀναίτιον) beyond Adam's primal abuse of his faculties, has nonetheless "caused" its own existential legacy in the human liability to passion (especially sexual passion), whence arise all kinds of sufferings. Pleasure has an absolute historical and existential priority to pain, not *vice versa*, though the two have become inexorably intertwined.

human, being composed just like us of an intellectual soul and a passible body, save only without sin (cf Heb 4:15). [89] His birth from a
woman within time was not preconditioned in any way by the pleasure derived from the transgression, but, in his love for humanity, he
willingly appropriated the pain which is the end of human nature,
the pain resulting from unrighteous pleasure. He did this in order
that, by suffering unjustly, he might uproot the principle of our
being conceived through unrighteous pleasure, which tyrannizes
our human nature. Moreover, he did it so that, with the Lord's own
death being not a penalty exacted for that principle of pleasure, like
other human beings, but rather a death specifically directed against
that principle, he might erase the just finality which human nature
encounters in death, since his own end did not have, as the cause of
its existence, the illicit pleasure on account of which he came and
which he subjected to his righteous punishment.

For in truth it was necessary that the Lord—who is by nature
wise and just and capable—not, in his wisdom, ignore the means of
curing us, nor, in his justice, arbitrarily save humanity when it had
fallen under sin by its own free will (γνώμη), nor, in his omnipo-
tence, falter in bringing the healing of humanity to completion. He
manifested the plan of his wisdom, then, in the manner in which he
cured humanity: by becoming a man without undergoing any kind
of change and alteration. He exhibited the equity of his justice in the
magnitude of his condescension, when he willingly (κατὰ θέλησιν)
submitted to the condemnation imposed on our passibility (τὸ
παθητόν) and turned that very passibility into an instrument for
eradicating sin and the death which is its consequence—or in other
words, for eradicating pleasure and the pain which is its consequence. For it was in human passibility that the power of sin and
death, the tyranny of sin connected with pleasure, and the oppres-
sion associated with pain all began. Indeed, the rule of pleasure and
pain over our nature clearly originated in the liability to passions.
Wanting to escape the oppressive experience of pain we sought
refuge in pleasure, attempting to console our nature when it was

hard-pressed with pain's torment. Striving to blunt pain's spasms with pleasure, [91] we merely sanctioned against ourselves a greater debt (cf Col 2:14) of pain, powerless to disconnect pleasure from pain and its toils. But the Lord exerted manifest strength of transcendent power by inaugurating for human nature a birth unchanged by the contrary realities (of pleasure and pain) which he himself experienced. For having given our human nature impassibility through his Passion,[6] remission through his toils, and eternal life through his death, he restored that nature again, renewing the habitudes of human nature by his own deprivations in the flesh and granting to human nature through his own incarnation the supernatural grace of deification.

In truth, then, God became a man and provided another beginning (ἀρχή), a second nativity (γένεσις), for human nature, which, through the vehicle of suffering, ends in the pleasure of the life to come. For Adam, our forefather, having transgressed God's commandment, introduced over against the original one another source of human generation based on pleasure and ending in the death that comes through suffering. On the serpent's advice, he conceived pleasure not as coming after an antecedent suffering but rather as terminating in suffering. And because of this unrighteous beginning based on pleasure, Adam subjected along with him his whole posterity, all who like him are born of the flesh, to the finality of death through suffering—and justly so. By contrast, our Lord became a man and in so doing fashioned for human nature another beginning, a second nativity through the Holy Spirit.[7] He even submitted to the death through suffering which in Adam's case was thoroughly justified, but which in his own case was absolutely unjust since it did not have as its genetic root the unrighteous pleasure stemming from

---

[6]For Maximus this is a sublime paradox, echoed also in *Mystagogia* 8, where he affirms that "in exchange for our passions [Christ] gives us his life-giving Passion as a salutary cure which saves the whole world" (PG 91:688C; trans. George Berthold, *Maximus Confessor: Selected Writings*, p. 198).

[7]Cf *Amb.* 42 (PG 91:1317A–C).

our forefather's disobedience. Therein the Lord destroyed both extremes—both the beginning and the end—of the mode of human generation inherited from Adam, such as were not originally of God's doing; and he liberated from liability to those extremes all who are mystically reborn by his Spirit and who no longer retain the pleasure of sexual conception derived from Adam, but retain only [93] the pain which Adam brought upon them—for this pain operates, not as a debt owed for sin, but according to the economy of salvation, because of the natural condition which counteracts sin: death. For death, once it has ceased having pleasure as its "birthmother"—that pleasure for which death itself became the natural punishment—clearly becomes the "father" of everlasting life. Indeed, just as Adam's life of pleasure became the mother of death and corruption, so too our Lord's death for Adam's sake, being free of the pleasure inherited from Adam, became the father of eternal life.

In my judgment, then, the scriptural text before us has rightly distinguished between, on the one hand, how human conception on the basis of pleasure, inherited from Adam, tyrannizes our nature, and feeds the death caused by pleasure, and, on the other hand, how the birth of our Lord in the flesh, based on his love of humanity, has done away both with the pleasure inherited from Adam and the death that he caused, and so erased Adam's punishment along with his sin. (For it was impossible for [the Lord's] conception, which was in no way connected with the [Adamic] beginning through which death came about as the finality, to succumb in the end to corruption through death). Now as I already said, the text before us has made a distinction. As long as only that which characterized Adam in his beginning and end—in his conception and corruption, I mean—oppressively ruled our human nature, it was not *the time for the judgment* leading toward the complete condemnation of sin *to begin.* But when the Word of God appeared to us in the flesh and became a perfect human being save only without sin (cf Heb 4:15), and willingly bore in the flesh only the punishment imposed on Adam's human nature; when he *judged sin in the flesh* (Rom 8:3) and innocently suffered, *the righteous for the unrighteous* (1 Pet 3:18), and converted the use (χρῆσις) of death, turning it into a condemnation of sin but not of human nature itself—[95] then was it *the time for the judgment* based upon this conversion of death and leading to the condemnation of sin *to begin.*

What I am saying is that in the beginning sin seduced Adam and persuaded him to transgress God's commandment, whereby sin gave rise to pleasure and, by means of this pleasure, nailed itself in Adam to the very depths (τῷ πυθμένι) of our nature,[8] thus condemning our whole human nature to death and, via humanity, pressing the nature of (all) created beings toward mortal extinction. For all this was contrived by the sower of sin and father of evil, the wicked Devil, who in his arrogance exiled himself from the glory of God and, in his envy both toward us and toward God, banished Adam from paradise in the attempt to destroy God's handiwork and to ruin what was basic to the origin of humankind. For the Devil, utterly defiled, is jealous not only of us for the glory before God that we may attain because of our virtue, but even jealous of God himself for the praiseworthy power he exercises over us for the sake of our salvation.

Therefore death in its dynasty dominates all of human nature because of the transgression, and has as the basis of its rule the pleasure which, through disobedience, initiated the whole of natural human conception—the pleasure on account of which this same death became the condemnation of our nature. But the Lord, when he became a man, did not have a birth in the flesh preceded by the unrighteous pleasure that caused death to be elicited as a punishment of our nature. He naturally willed to die, to take on death amid the passibility of his human nature. Clearly he suffered, and converted the use (χρῆσις) of death so that in him it would be a

[8]On Maximus's highly qualified understanding of "original sin," see Jean-Claude Larchet, "Ancestral Guilt according to St. Maximus the Confessor: A Bridge between Eastern and Western Conceptions," *Sobornost* 20 (1998): 26–48; and John Boojamra, "Original Sin according to St. Maximus the Confessor," *St Vladimir's Theological Quarterly* 20 (1976): 19–30.

condemnation not of our nature but manifestly only of sin itself.[9] For it was impossible for death to become a condemnation in one whose birth was not based on pleasure. His death could only be the destruction of our forefather's sin, which caused the fear of death to rule human nature.[10] If in Adam death was a condemnation of his nature that began with the pleasure of his own childbearing, it is for good reason that in Christ death has become a condemnation of sin, wherewith our nature has recovered in Christ [97] a birth free of pleasure. In turn, just as in Adam sin, based on pleasure, condemned our nature to corruption through death, and occasioned the *time* (καιρός) for our nature to be condemned to death because of its sin, so too in Christ, on the basis of his righteousness, human nature condemns sin through death and inaugurates the *time* for sin to be condemned to death because of righteousness.[11] At this point our nature is thoroughly ridded of birth through pleasure, for it was in view of this birth that death, like a debt owed by everyone, necessarily accompanied our condemnation. And so in Adam this very death is a condemnation of human nature because of sin, but in Christ it is a condemnation of sin because of his righteousness. For the one who because of sin suffers in the resulting condemnation of nature justly endures death, but Christ, who does not suffer because of sin

[9]Maximus repeats here his slightly earlier affirmation that Christ "converted the *use* of death" (τὴν τοῦ θανάτου χρῆσιν ἀντέστρεψιν) so as to condemn sin and not human nature itself. We already see in *Ad Thal.* 42 (translated above) Maximus's larger perspective on Christ's assumption of human passibility in its fullness, becoming the "sin" which is a consequence of the fall (but not the "sin" committed in moral acts) and so for our sakes taking on the mortality which is its condemnation. Recalling here the christianized Stoic idiom of "good use" of the human passions (cf *Ad Thal.* 1), Maximus describes Christ "using" death, the ultimate "passion" and the end of human passibility, as a redemptive instrument.

[10]Elsewhere, Maximus speaks of Christ's blameless *use* of the fear of death (*Disputation with Pyrrhus*, PG 91:297B), for Christ alone turns it into a "voluntary" fear that encourages the Christian faithful in their own confrontation with death (*Opusc.* 7, PG 91:80D; cf *Comm. on the Lord's Prayer*, CCSG 23:34, 135–35, 142).

[11]Throughout this section of his argument, Maximus is continuing to refer back to the original text in question, concerning the "time (καιρός) . . . for judgment . . . to begin" (1 Pet 4:17). (The word time [καιρός] is thus italicized throughout the translation).

but instead bestows his grace on human nature in the economy of salvation, looks to condemn sin and willingly submits to the death caused by sin in order to destroy sin.

Because of Adam, who by his disobedience gave rise both to the law of birth through pleasure and the death of our nature which was its condemnation, all of his posterity who come into existence according to this law of birth through pleasure are necessarily sub-ject—even if unwilling—to the death that is functionally linked with this birth and serves to condemn our nature. It was *time* for human nature to be condemned for its sin, while the law of birth through pleasure was ruling our nature. By contrast, because of Christ, who completely divested his human nature of the law of birth through pleasure, and who willingly took up the use (χρῆσις) of death—which on Adam's account had condemned human nature—solely for purposes of condemning sin, all who in the Spirit are willingly reborn of Christ *with the bath of regeneration* (Titus 3:5) are able by grace to put off their original Adamic birth based on pleasure. By keeping the gospel commandments they preserve the baptismal grace of sinlessness and the unabated and immaculate power of mystical [99] adoption in the Spirit.[12] For good reason, then, those thus regenerated enjoy the effective use of death for purposes of con-demning sin. For them the *time* (καιρός) has come to condemn sin in the flesh: generally speaking, the very time which, in the context of graced nature, began with the incarnation of the Word for the sake of the great mystery of God becoming a man; yet particularly speaking, in the context of graced activity, it is that time beginning when each one, through baptism, receives the grace of adoption. Thus adopted, all those who by keeping the commandments of their own free will (γνωμικῶς) enjoy only birth in the Spirit uphold the use of death, a use occasioned them by scores of sufferings, to con-demn sin. For it is no longer because of sin that one who is baptized and who guards that baptism, which is reinforced by keeping God's

[12]On Maximus's doctrine of baptismal adoption, see *Ad Thal.* 6 (translated above, pp. 103–4).

commandments, spurns death as a debt owed for sin; rather, the baptized acquires the use of death to condemn sin, which in turn mystically leads that person to divine and unending life. Such will ensue if indeed the saints, for the sake of truth and righteousness, have virtuously finished the course of this life with its many sufferings, liberating their nature within themselves from death as a condemnation of sin and, like Christ, the *captain of our salvation* (Heb 2:10), turned death from a weapon to destroy human nature into a weapon to destroy sin. For if sin maintains death as a weapon to destroy human nature in those who, with Adam, keep sin active, how much more will human nature boast death as a weapon to destroy sin in those who realize righteousness through faith in Christ![13]

So beginning with the mystery of God's becoming human, when the incarnate God fully removed—in those who with him are born in the Spirit—that birth which subjected our nature to the law of pleasure, *the time* arrived, as I said, *for the judgment of the house of God to begin.* It is the time for sin to be condemned, the time when sin begins to be condemned amid the sufferings endured by those who have come to believe and know the truth and who, through baptism, have put off the birth based on pleasure. [101] For the text is referring to these faithful ones as the *house of God,* just as elsewhere the most divine Apostle Paul says that Christ was faithful over God's house, and we are his house (Heb 3:6).[14] Moreover Peter himself, the chief of apostles, affirms the same when he asks further in our text, *If we are to be judged first, then what will be the end of those who disobey the gospel of God?* (1 Pet 4:17b) It is as if he were asking: If we who are deemed worthy to become the *house of God* by grace through the Spirit are obliged to demonstrate so great a patience amid suffering for the sake of righteousness and for the purpose of

---

[13]Maximus is insistent that the Christian appropriates Christ's own good "use" of the ultimate passion of death (see note 9 above) by his or her own discipline of mortification. One should not overlook his important distinction between destroying death and *destroying sin through the instrumentality of death.*

[14]Like many patristic authors, Maximus assumed that Paul was the author of the anonymous Epistle to the Hebrews.

condemning sin; and if, while the evildoers hold death in contempt, we, being virtuous, are obliged to embrace death eagerly, *then what will be the end of those who disobey the gospel of God?* In other words, what sort of end or judgment awaits those who have not only kept alive and active—both in soul and in body, both in will (γνώμη) and in nature—the Adamic birth based on pleasure, but who embrace neither our God and Father, who appeals to them through his incarnate Son, nor the Mediator and Son himself, who acts as an ambassador for the Father, and who was himself willingly sent, by the Father's counsel, to reconcile us to the Father, to die for our sake, so that in himself he might glorify us, illuminate us with his beauty and his own divinity, precisely to the extent that, because of us, he submitted to being dishonored by our sufferings? This, it seems to me, is the *gospel of God*: that the incarnate Son is God's ambassador and advocate for humanity, and has earned reconciliation to the Father for those who yield to him for the deification that is without origin.[15]

For this reason the great Apostle Peter inveighs against the unyielding when he furthermore asks, *And if the righteous man is scarcely saved, where will the impious man* [103] *and the sinner appear?* (1 Pet 4:18; = Prov 11:31, LXX). Most likely he is calling the *righteous man* one who is faithful and who guards the grace bestowed in baptism, one who, through scores of sufferings, has preserved unabated his adoption through the Spirit. The *salvation* of which he speaks is the fullest grace of deification bestowed on the worthy and utterly attained by one who clings to divine realities at the highest level. The *impious man*, the *sinner*, can only be the one who is alien to the grace of the gospel: *impious* because he has no

---

[15]This curious allusion to the "deification without origin" (ἀγένητος θέωσις) prompts the scholiast of the *Ad Thalassium* (possibly Maximus himself, some have surmised) to add the following explanatory note: "With the 'deification without beginning' he is referring to the specific illumination subsisting within God's divinity (ἡ κατ' εἶδος ἐνυπόστατον τῆς θεότητος ἔλλαμψις), which has no origin but appears as incomprehensible (ἀνεννόητος) in those who are worthy of it" (CCSG 22:111, 71–73).

faith in Christ, a *sinner* because the birth inherited from his ancient (Adamic) origins is alive and well in him in the corruption of the passions. Or perhaps the text is calling *impious* the one who is wholly bereft only of the knowledge of Christ, and *sinner* the one who has faith but, like me, transgresses the gospel commandments which keep clean the tunic of incorruptibility given us through holy baptism. Their status (θέσις)—that of the *impious* and the *sinner*, I mean—is made known to those who exercise some measure of diligence in acquiring mystical knowledge. For the text's mention of *where* (ποῦ) they will be clearly indicates a position not lacking in local parameters. And if indeed the status of the righteous is distinguished from that of sinners, the righteous man will not be in a status of *where* at all, having by grace received God himself as his status instead of a local *where*; such is God's promise. For God does not admit of *where*; he is unqualifiedly beyond all *where*. In him will be the sure foundation of all who are saved, as testified in scripture: *Be to me a protecting God, and a stronghold to save me* (Ps 70:3, LXX). Whosoever does not share in the power of well-being in relation to God will be like a body part utterly bereft of the soul's vital energy.

[105] Or in yet another sense, since the location (τόπος) of the saved will be God himself, who is incomprehensible, unlimited by time and space, and infinite, *becoming all things to all men* (1 Cor 9:22) in proportion to their righteousness, or rather granting himself to each person according to the measure of what they have suffered, in full knowledge, for the sake of righteousness (just as the soul reveals itself as active in the parts of the body according to the capacity underlying each part, maintaining in itself the existence of the parts and sustaining them for life), then *where will the impious man and the sinner appear?* For *where* will one who is unable to receive the effective presence of God in a state of well-being *appear* after having endured exclusion from the divine life, a life transcending aeon, time, and place?

So we have two options. According to our first interpretation, by way of affirmation (καταφατικῶς), in considering *where will the impious man and the sinner appear?* we can say that he will by no means be free of a life constrained within limits, since he will not enjoy that life which fully defies limitation and is beyond any location. Or, according to our second interpretation, by way of negation (ἀποφατικῶς), there is no *where* for him to appear, since he does not enjoy God as sustaining his life unto well-being. Either way, *how* will he exist when he does not have God as his location itself, the only sure foundation of well-being, which is in God? Simply stated, if, after much vexation, *the righteous man will be saved*, what will there be or what will become of the one who gives no account of piety or virtue in the present life?

AD THALASSIUM 64

On the Prophet Jonah and the Economy of Salvation

(CCSG 22:187–241)

Q. [187] What kind of sense can be made of the statement in the prophet Jonah concerning Nineveh which reads: . . . *in which more than twelve myriads of men dwell, who do not know their right hand from their left* . . . (Jon 4:11)? I ask this because I do not find anything edifying in its literal sense. For it speaks not of children, such that I would think of infants, but of *men.* What kind of man, being of a sound mind, is ignorant of his right hand or left? Explain for me who these *men* are, and what the *right hand* and the *left hand* signify according to an anagogical interpretation.

R. None of the persons, places, times, or other things recorded in Scripture—animate and inanimate, sensible and intelligible—has its concurrent literal or spiritual meanings rendered always according to the same interpretive mode. Whoever, therefore, is infallibly trained in the divine knowledge of Holy Scripture must, for the diversity of what appears and is communicated therein, interpret each recorded thing in a different way and assign it, according to its place or time, the fitting spiritual meaning.[1] For the name of each thing signified in

[1]In *Amb.* 37 (PG 91:1293A–1296D), Maximus undertakes the scientific analysis of ten progressive modes (τρόποι) through which the spiritual meaning of things (πράγματα) in Scripture is to be discerned, beginning with the five basic categories

145

Scripture lends itself to many meanings by the potency of the Hebrew language.[2] Clearly we find this to be the case here.

The name Jonah can be translated according to various pronunciations [of the Hebrew]: "repose of God," "gift of God," "healing from God," "God's grace to them," "labor of God," "dove," "flight from beauty," and "their toil."[3] Moreover, Jonah went into *Joppa*, into the *sea*, into the *whale*, into *Nineveh*, and under the *gourd plant*. *Joppa* is variously translated [189] "vision of joy," "wondrous beauty," and "powerful joy." Therefore Jonah the prophet is a figure of Adam, of our shared human nature, of Christ, of prophetic grace, and of the ungrateful Jewish people who toil over everything good and are perpetually jealous of the graces of God.[4]

For example, Jonah is a figure of Adam and of our shared human nature when he flees Joppa to the sea, for which reason he is called "flight from beauty" by the intrinsic force of his name. Joppa in itself clearly constitutes a figure of paradise, which truly is, and is rightly called, a "vision of joy," a "powerful joy," and a "wondrous beauty"

of "place" (τόπος), "time" (χρόνος), "race" (γένος), "individual persona" (πρόσωπον), and "dignity" (ἀξία) or "occupation" (ἐπιτηδεύμα). See Paul M. Blowers, "The World in the Mirror of Holy Scripture: Maximus the Confessor's Short Hermeneutical Treatise in *Ambiguum ad Joannem* 37," in *In Dominico Eloquio—In Lordly Eloquence: Essays on Patristic Exegesis in Honor of Robert Louis Wilken*, ed. Paul M. Blowers, Angela Russell Christman, David G. Hunter, and Robin Darling Young (Grand Rapids: Eerdmans, 2002), pp. 408–26.

[2] On Maximus's important teaching on the possibility of multiple meanings of a given scriptural text, see Blowers, *Exegesis and Spiritual Pedagogy*, pp. 185–92.

[3] Maximus is undoubtedly depending here on earlier patristic onomastics, where Hebrew names or words were etymologically broken down and reconstructed to show multiple semanatic possibilities. He produces a similar onomastic analysis of "Zorobabel" (Zerubbabel) in *Ad Thal.* 54 (CCSG 7:443, 10–445, 39). See also Blowers, *Exegesis and Spiritual Pedagogy*, pp. 203–11.

[4] Maximus here proposes an enormous range of interpretive possibilities through the prospective combination of the eight *translations* of "Jonah" multiplied by the five *situations* in which Jonah finds himself and the four *typoi* of Jonah. Yet in what follows we find Maximus exploiting only a limited number of these combinations. See Carl Laga, "Maximi Confessoris *ad Thalassium Quaestio* 64," in *After Chalcedon: Studies in Theology and Church History Offered to Professor Albert Van Roey for His Seventieth Birthday*, ed. Carl Laga, J.A. Munitz, and L. van Rompay, Orientalia lovaniensia analecta 18 (Leuven: Departement Oriëntalistiek, 1985), pp. 203–15.

because of the abundance of incorruptibility within it. Whatever this paradise may have been, it was planted by the hand of God. For, as Scripture says, *The Lord planted a garden in Eden, and placed there the man whom he had formed* (Gen 2:8). He also planted certain trees in the garden that were either visible to the eye or else intelligible, and the tree of life, which was in the middle of the garden. Adam was commanded to eat of all the trees but perhaps did not touch them [in a sensible way]. For the text says, *you may eat from every tree in the garden* (Gen 2:18).

Now *Joppa* can also signify virtue and knowledge, and the wisdom based on both: virtue when it is translated "wondrous beauty"; knowledge when translated "vision of joy"; and wisdom when it means "powerful joy" since, when man is perfected in wisdom, he acquires unspeakable joy, a potent joy able to maintain him with a godly and divine sustenance. For according to Scripture, *wisdom is a tree of life to those who lay hold of her, and she is a secure help for those who rely on her, as on the Lord* (Prov 3:18). Just as Adam absconded paradise by his disobedience, we should observe how our human nature is always fleeing Joppa (that is, the habitude of virtue and [191] knowledge, and the grace of wisdom based on them both) because its intelligence is thoroughly engrossed in wickedness. And like our forefather Adam, who, when he lapsed, was tossed from paradise into this world, so too our nature willingly was dragged down into the *sea* (the brine of sin, I mean), where it both bears, and is born along in, the unstable, helter-skelter delusion and confusion of material things[5]—even attending diligently to them. The more those who cling to this error and confusion profit from it, the deeper they are merely plunged [into the brine of sin] and swallowed by the *whale* and *enveloped with water up to the soul;* the more too they are *engulfed by the deepest abyss,* and their *head sinks into the clefts of the mountains,* and they descend *into the earth, whose bars are its eternal*

[5]The image of "bearing" and "being born along" in the chaos of material existence has already been seen in *Amb.* 8 (PG 91:1101D–1104B; and above, pp. 75–8) and *Amb.* 42 (PG 91:1348D; and above, p. 95).

constraints (Jon 2:6–7). For it is obvious that the *earth*—the truly *dark and gloomy earth, the earth of eternal darkness* (Job 10:21)—is like the depths of the deepest abyss. In it, says the great Job, who struggled with great ordeals for the sake of truth, *there is no light, nor can one see any life of mortal beings* (Job 10:22).

The prophet Jonah therefore signifies Adam, or our shared human nature, by bearing in himself mystically a figure of the following. Human nature has slipped from divine benefits, as from *Joppa*, and has descended, as though into a *sea*, into the misery of the present life, and been plunged into the chaotic and roaring waters of attachment to material objects. It has been swallowed whole by the *whale*, that spiritual and insatiable beast the Devil himself. It has been *enveloped with water* all around it, the water of temptations to evil, *up to the soul*, in the sense that human life has been submerged with temptations. So too our nature has been *engulfed in the deepest abyss*, that is to say, it has been imprisoned by the complete [193] ignorance of the mind and the overwhelming of rational thinking by the sheer pressure of vice. Our nature's *head* has *sunk into the clefts of the mountains* in the sense that its primary principle of unity by faith vis-à-vis the Monad is like the head of the entire body of the virtues, which has become confined within the machinations of the wicked powers, as in the dark clefts of mountains, and been dashed into a multiplicity of errant beliefs and illusions. For the scriptural text calls *clefts of mountains* the delusional designs of the spirits of wickedness who hover in the depths of the *deepest abyss* of ignorance. Human nature has descended *into the earth, whose bars are its eternal constraints*, that is, it has fallen into a virtual desert of all divine sensibility, where its disposition has been deprived of the vital activity of virtue, and where it has no sense at all of goodness nor any active desire of the mind for God. The darkness of ignorance and the unimaginable depth of evil have come over human nature like an *abyss*, and the *mountains* of error—meaning the *spirits of wickedness* (Eph 6:12)—have rooted themselves on it. Receptive to their deceit and vice, human nature, having originally entered the

clefts of the mountains, later became, with its utterly wicked disposition, their very foundation. Like *eternal bars*, human nature has
ingrained proclivities toward material objects which keep the mind
from being freed from the darkness of ignorance to behold the light
of true knowledge. As I said a little earlier, the great Job is perhaps
referring to such an evil disposition when he speaks enigmatically of
the *dark and gloomy earth, the earth of eternal darkness* (Job 10:21). It
is *dark* because it is barren of all true knowledge and contemplation,
gloomy because it is void of all virtue and ascetic practice. In it, says
Job, *there is no light*—no light, that is, of knowledge and truth— *nor
can one see any life of mortal beings* (Job 10:22)—clearly referring to
what is the proper way of life for rational beings.

[195] Perhaps he happened into these circumstances because,
being in himself a figure of the passions of humanity, the prophet
Jonah was mercifully preparing humanity itself for the same, taking
on himself what is common to our human nature. So the meaning
of his name, when translated "flight from beauty," is suitably adapted
to one who was a figure of Adam. On the other hand, when Jonah
prefigures the God who for our sake became like us, through flesh
animated by a rational soul, save only without sin (Heb 4:15), he
marks out in advance the mystery of the incarnation and the sufferings that accompanied it. He signifies the descent from heaven into
this world in his transit from *Joppa* into the *sea*. His being swallowed
by the whale and his impassible submission for three days and three
nights indicates the mystery of Christ's death, burial, and resurrection (cf Mt 12:40). Thus his name can fittingly be translated "repose
of God," "healing from God," and "God's grace to them." And perhaps he is rightly called "labor of God" because of his voluntary
suffering. For by his own actions the prophet mystically prefigures
the authentic "repose" of those who have labored amid physical
pain, the "healing" of those who have been broken, the "grace" of
the forgiveness of sins—our God Jesus Christ. For our Lord and
God himself became a man and entered into the *sea* of life like
ours, insofar as he descended from the heaven of *Joppa* (translated

"contemplation of joy") into the ocean of this life. As Scripture says, he is the one *who for the joy that was set before him endured the cross, despising the shame* (Heb 12:2). He even descended willingly into the heart of the *earth*, where the Evil One had swallowed us through death, and drew us up by his resurrection, leading our whole captive nature up to heaven. Truly he is our "repose," our "healing," our "grace": our repose since, with his timely human life, he freed the law from the situation of its carnal bondage; our healing since, [197] by his resurrection, he cured us of the destruction wrought by death and corruption; our grace insofar as he distributes adoption in the Spirit by our God and Father through faith, and the grace of deification to each who is worthy. For it was necessary, necessary in truth, for him to become the light unto that *earth* (cf Jn 1:9), to be the power of our God and Father (cf 1 Cor 1:18) in the earth with its abiding darkness and *eternal bars*, so that, having dispelled the darkness of ignorance—being the Father's light, as it were—and having crushed the *bars* of evil insofar as he is the concrete (ἐνυπόστατος) power of God, he might wondrously liberate human nature from its bondage to these things under the Evil One, and endow it with the inextinguishable light of true knowledge and the indefatigable power of the virtues.

Furthermore, when the prophet Jonah mystically leaves Joppa, he constitutes in himself a figure of prophetic grace transferring from the *Joppa* of corporeal observance of the law, originally considered glorious, over to the Gentiles by way of the gospel, leaving the Jewish people barren of joy because of their unbelief. He represents as well the Church of the Gentiles, which, like Nineveh, has turned to God amid numerous tribulations, dangers, adversities, sufferings, persecutions, and deaths.[6] He signifies that prophetic

6See Yves-Marie Duval, *Le livre de Jonas dans la littérature chrétienne grecque et latine* (Paris: Études Augustiniennes, 1973), vol. 2, pp. 381–5. Duval notes Maximus's partial dependence on Gregory Nazianzen in his interpretation of Jonah, but highlights as well the Confessor's unique contributions, among them his depiction of Jonah himself as a *typos* of "prophetic grace." Duval faults Maximus for ignoring the true sin of Jonah in repudiating God's call when he departed Joppa, and thus

grace which distinctly abandons the cult of the law and enters the *sea* of unsolicited adversities, the flood of upsurging persecutions, and the struggles, sufferings, and dangers therein, and so is swallowed by the *whale* of death, yet by no means completely destroyed. For there is nothing in creation capable of impeding the advance of the grace proclaimed evangelically to the Gentiles: neither *tribulation*, nor *distress*, nor *persecution*, nor *famine*, nor *danger*, nor *sword* (Rom 8:35). On the contrary, grace was confirmed by these very circumstances, and subdued everything which arose against it. Even amid suffering, grace all the more conquered those who suffered, [199] and turned our errant nature toward the true and living God, just as Jonah turned Nineveh toward him. Even if the Evil One appears to conceal grace amid the torrent of persecution, as the whale concealed the prophet Jonah, he was nevertheless unable ultimately to hold grace in check, and remains unable to alter the strength of God's ability to activate his grace. For this reason the Evil One caused the grace rather to be manifested even more distinctly in its disciples after they experienced opposition, and the more he did this, the more he undermined his own power in the attempt. He beheld for himself not only the utter impregnability of grace, but the physical weakness of the saints who proclaim that grace to the Gentiles (cf 2 Cor 12:9), the weakness which itself became a force capable of destroying his power and utterly destroying *every proud obstacle to the knowledge of God* (2 Cor 10:5). He saw too that this grace is rendered even stronger spiritually by the apparent capitulation of the body to abuse.

Paul, that great trumpeter of truth who learned this very fact from his own experience of suffering, and who lived in the *newness of the Spirit* rather than the *obsoleteness of the letter* (Rom 7:6), having become a servant of the prophetic grace in Christ for the Gentiles, says that *we have this treasure in earthen vessels* (2 Cor 4:7). He

deviating from the literal sense cherished by many earlier authors in the patristic tradition. Yet Maximus simply presupposes that the recorded events, as prefigurations, hold their own transcending spiritual sense for the admonition of the Church (cf 1 Cor 10:11).

is calling the word of grace a *treasure* and this passible body of ours an *earthen vessel.* Or else the *vessel* may be seen as the alleged vulgarity of Paul's outward speech which nonetheless conquered all the wisdom of this world (cf 2 Cor 11:6; 1 Cor 2:1–5), or which, to the extent it was containable, contained the wisdom of God inaccessible to this world, and filled the entire inhabited earth with its light of true knowledge—*in order,* as Paul says, *to show that the transcendent power belongs to God and not to us. We are afflicted in every way but not crushed; perplexed, but not driven to despair; persecuted, but not forsaken; downcast, but not destroyed. We always carry in the body the death of Jesus, so that the life of* [201] *Jesus may also be manifested in our bodies. For as long as we live we are constantly being consigned to death for Jesus's sake, so that the life of Jesus may be made manifest in our mortal flesh. So death is at work in us, but life is at work in you* (2 Cor 4:7–12). Those who innocently endure death amid voluntary sufferings for the sake of truth, and who have become heralds of the message of grace, continue to bring about life in the Spirit for the Gentiles through knowledge of the truth. Such is precisely what Jonah did as well when, mystically prefiguring this same grace in his own person, he suffered and endured these kinds of perils in order to turn the Ninevites from their sin to God. This is why the name Jonah, by its inherent force, can also appropriately be translated "gift of God" and "labor of God." For the prophetic grace toward the Gentiles is commended both as a gift of God—indeed a beloved and philanthropic gift—and as God's labor: God's gift since it bestows the light of true knowledge, and furnishes an incorruptible life for those who receive it; God's labor because it convinces its servants to take pride in their own labors on behalf of truth, and teaches those who are too anxious about their life in the flesh to extend themselves more through suffering than through remission of suffering. To such as these, grace makes the natural weakness of the flesh in the face of suffering the basis of a transcendent spiritual power.

For the message of grace which, through multiple testings, communicates itself to human nature, or to the Church of the Gentiles—

just as Jonah went to the great city of Nineveh by way of considerable tribulations—has persuaded the ruling law of nature to arise from its *throne* (that is, from its former [203] habit of inclining toward evil in its subservience to the senses), to remove its *robe* (in other words, to put off the vanity of worldly glory), to put on *sackcloth* (indicating contrition and the annoying, astringent discipline of mortification befitting a godly way of life), and to sit upon *ashes* (that is, the voluntary poverty of spirit, upon which sits everyone who has been instructed in living a pious life and who has the scourge of conscience torturing him about his sins) (Jon 3:5–7). The word of grace, when it is proclaimed, not only persuades the *king* (the law of nature) but men—human beings who together compose human nature—as well, fully convincing them to confess and faithfully to proclaim that the one God is the Creator and Judge of the universe. So too it prepares them completely to renounce their former evil ways and, *from the least to the greatest of them* (Jon 3:5), to *don sackcloth* (meaning, that is, to pursue earnestly the mortification of the passions). I surmise that, according to the anagogical interpretation, the *least* and the *greatest* ones here refer respectively to those who have been convicted by the word of living in lesser and greater degrees of wickedness.

The text reads: *And the men of Nineveh believed God, and proclaimed a fast, and donned sackcloth, from the least to the greatest of them. And the word reached the king of Nineveh, and he arose from his throne, removed his robe, put on sackcloth, and sat on ashes. And the king and his nobles issued a proclamation and had it announced in Nineveh, saying, "Let no men, cattle, oxen, or sheep taste or eat anything or drink any water"* (Jon 3:5–7). The *king*, as I said, is the law of nature, and his captains here are the rational, irascible, and [205] concupiscible faculties of the soul.[7] The *men* of this *city* (of human

[7]Maximus frequently uses this psychological image in developing moral or spiritual interpretations of Old Testament war narratives. In *Ad Thal.* 49 (CCSG 7:355, 68–89), for example, he expands at length on King Hezekiah (1 Chr 32:2–4) as a figure of the mind (νοῦς) with his "elders" and "captains" as the three principal faculties of

nature, that is) are, by one interpretation, those who falter in their reasoning and who cling to an errant knowledge of God and of divine realities. The *cattle* are those who, by their concupiscence, fall completely into sin and so bear the burden of pleasure with their bodily sufferings. The *oxen* are those who squander the entire function of their irascibility on acquiring earthly things; for they say that drinking the blood of the ox causes the drinker to die instantly, and clearly blood is a symbol of irascibility. They furthermore say that the *sheep*, culpable indeed, are those who, bereft of understanding, graze on the "pasture" of the contemplation of visible things by sense alone and with a view to passion. For we surmise that, in this passage of Scripture, all were considered culpable until the word (of grace) took hold of them and changed them for the better. This is why the text goes on to say, *let (no one) eat anything or drink any water* (Jon 3:7), thus forestalling the original root causes of the passions in each of these culpable denizens just mentioned. Thus undermining the causes of passion, the text further portrays the amelioration of those once entangled in wicked ways when it further adds, *and the men and cattle were clothed in sackcloth, and cried out earnestly to God; and each one turned from his wicked way and from the iniquity in his hands* (Jon 3:8). As I said already, we understand *men* here to refer to those ensnared in rational judgment staggered by diseases of the soul. The *cattle* include those who, by abusing their irascible and concupiscible faculties in the interest of pleasure, remain bound by bodily sufferings; all who don, like *sackcloth*, the mortification of earthly concerns (cf Col 3:5), that is, of every earthly standard and purpose; and those who *cry out earnestly* (that is, with a loud voice), or in other words, those who [207] in their bold stand against licentiousness, openly proclaim their freedom from former sins; those who put off, like a *(wicked) way*, their habitual behavior and the iniquity operative in their actions as though in their *hands*.

the soul (rational, concupiscible, irascible) called to stabilize the soul in its desire for God and practice of virtue.

So then *Nineveh,* being interpreted as our shared human nature, or as the Church of the Gentiles, shows up Jonah (that is, the word of prophetic grace) preaching within its precincts and turning sinners to God every single day. But if we interpret *Nineveh* specifically as each individual's contemplation, we would say that the *great city* is the soul of each and every person to which, in its transgression, the word of God is sent preaching repentance unto life (cf Jon 3:1–4). In turn we may interpret the *king* of that *city,* or soul, as the mind (νοῦς) and its captains as the soul's innate faculties. The *men,* then, signify impassioned thoughts, the *cattle* movements of the concupiscible faculty in relation to the body, the *oxen* covetous functions of the irascible faculty toward material objects, and the *sheep* the attempts of the senses to grasp sensible objects without intelligent reflection. So too the *king* is the mind that arises, as from its *throne,* from the habitude born of its former ignorance; the mind that puts off, like a *robe,* a false estimation of created beings; the mind that puts on the *sackcloth* of repentance for its evil affectations and that sits upon the *ashes* of a habitude reflecting the poverty of the spirit; the mind that commands its *men, cattle, oxen,* and *sheep* to abstain from the food of wickedness or the drink of ignorance (that is, to desist from evil deeds and from contemplation rendered errant by its subservience to sense), and enjoins them as well to don *sackcloth* (meaning a habitude that mortifies unnatural passions while preserving virtue and knowledge); the mind that commands them to *cry out to God earnestly,* which clearly indicates fervently confessing their former sins, propitiating with humility him who is able to grant forgiveness for their former ways, and asking him who readily bestows, on those who ask, the [209] realization of morally superior pursuits and the preservation of the power of free choice in a morally immutable state; the mind that enjoins them to keep the mind from the *evil way* of its former error and to put off, from the soul's practical faculties, the habitude that conceives of wickedness.

Within this *great city*—interpreted either as our shared human nature, the Church of the Gentiles, or the individual soul that has been saved through the word of virtue and knowledge or of faith and a pure conscience—there dwell *more than twelve myriads of men who do not know their right hand or their left* (Jon 4:11). By an anagogical interpretation, I surmise that by the *twelve myriads* Scripture is referring to the principles (λόγοι) of time and nature, or more precisely the knowledge which cannot comprehend visible nature apart from those principles. For if the number "twelve" is the sum of five and seven—human nature containing the "five" senses and time being divided in weeks of "seven"—then the number twelve obviously indicates nature and time. Yet the text speaks figuratively of *more than twelve myriads* of men in order for us to know that this limited number is transcended by the many more who, unseen here, constitute a quantity over and beyond the number twelve.

Therefore it is the wholly blessed Church of God that contains *more than twelve myriads of men who do not know their right hand or their left*—those, namely, who in their virtue and knowledge have gone beyond the principles of time and nature and passed over to the magnificence of eternal and noetic realities. For whoever, by reason of his genuine virtue, forgets the passions of the flesh on his "left," and who, because of his impeccable knowledge, does not succumb to the disease of a growing conceit over his accomplishments on his "right," becomes a man who *does not know his right hand* (or does not, as it were, long for fleeting glory) *or his left hand* (or is not, as it were, roused by carnal [211] passions). It seems, then, that the Word is presumably calling vainglory about one's achievements the *right hand*, and intemperance with respect to shameful passions the *left hand.*

Moreover, every individual soul illumined by visions of spiritual realities also has these *men who do not know their right hand or their left.* For every soul that withdraws its intellectual power from contemplating nature and time contains, like *men*, natural thoughts (λογισμοί) that exceed the number *twelve*, or in other words, thoughts that are henceforth no longer labored by the principles of things subject to nature and time, but engage in comprehending and knowing divine mysteries.[8] Such thoughts, in this sense, *do not know their right hand or their left.* For the rational knowledge of the virtues, or in other words, the true and active recognition of the cause of the virtues, induces the soul completely to ignore the two extremes of excess and defect that lie on either side—like the *right hand* and the *left hand*—of the mean of the virtues.[9]

For if by its very nature there is nothing irrational in reason, then whoever is elevated to the rational principle of the virtues acknowledges no position at all for the irrational. For it is impossible to contemplate opposite realities both at the same time, and to perceive the one as appearing simultaneously with the other. If there is no principle of infidelity in faith, and if light is by nature not a cause of darkness, and if the Devil cannot exhibit himself together with Christ, then clearly nothing at all irrational coexists with reason. And if nothing irrational can by any means coexist with reason, then whoever is elevated to the rational principle of the virtues does not, as I said, acknowledge any position for the irrational, since he knows virtue alone, and knows it as it is, not as it is alleged to be. This is why he knows neither the *right hand* through excess nor the *left hand* through defect; for he plainly sees irrationality on both sides of him. For if reason is the limit and measure of created beings, then being moved contrary to (παρά) that [213] limit and measure, or else beyond (ὑπέρ) that limit and measure, is tantamount to irrationality and therefore irrational. For both alike cause those so moved to deviate from what truly and properly exists. The one [being moved beyond reason's limit and measure] induces them to pursue a course that is obscure and limitless, a movement which, because of a lack of

[8]Particularly in his close study of Evagrius's ascetic teaching, Maximus was already quite familiar with the notion of idle or disturbing "thoughts" (λογισμοί) of the undisciplined mind; but here he clearly indicates that not all λογισμοί are intrinsically evil or laden with passions. The mind must aspire to *natural* "thoughts" worthy of the contemplation of divine mysteries.

[9]On excess (ὑπερβολή), defect (ἔλλειψις), and mean (μεσότης) in the practice of the virtues, cf Aristotle, *Nicomachean Ethics* 1106B. This notion was a commonplace of Christian ethical teaching by Maximus's time.

intellectual definition, does not have as its object the God who is already the preconceived goal of their movement; in this case they are formed ever further to the right. But the other [being moved contrary to reason's limit and measure] induces them to pursue a course contrary to their purpose, in the direction of sense experience alone, because, in their lack of intellectual tenacity, they think that their preconceived goal is confined within the realm of their senses. Whoever ignores these aberrations and does not succumb to them fixes himself solely to the rational principle of virtue, confining all functioning of his intellectual power to that principle; and thus he is able to think upon nothing beyond reason or contrary to reason.

And yet if someone ambitious wishes his mind to aspire to a more sublime meaning, he will interpret the *right hand* wholly as the principles of incorporeal things, and the *left hand* those of corporeal things. Whoever's mind has been absolutely elevated to the Cause of created beings is fully ignorant of both, since he does not contemplate any principle within God, who is by essence beyond every principle as far as all causality is concerned. Such a mind, having been drawn toward God and away from all created beings, knows none of the *logoi* of the things from which it has withdrawn; in its ineffable vision it knows only that Logos whom it approaches by grace.

God is able to spare these and suchlike human beings and, on their account, the whole world of *men* who truly *do not know* their culpable *right hand* or *left* (since nearly everything in Scripture is interpreted in terms of praise and blame). Even if the envious Jewish people, that thoughtless, ungrateful, and misanthropic people, hostile to the love of humankind, laboring over the salvation of humanity [215] and thus daring to fight against the very goodness of God, is cut to pieces, it renounces life and considers the salvation of the Gentiles in Christ an occasion for sorrow.[10] In its folly, the Jewish people

[10]What follows is one of Maximus's more passionate diatribes against the Jews in the *Ad Thalassium*. In the light of fresh tensions between the Jewish and Christian communities in North Africa in the early seventh century, Carl Laga ("Maximi Confessoris *ad Thalassium Quaestio* 64," p. 215) surmises that the Confessor's invective may arise from actual debates over the Bible renewed between Christian and Jewish theologians.

esteems the *gourd plant* far above the salvation of the Gentiles, and grieves when it sees the gourd withered by the *worm* (Jon 4:6–9). Now I said earlier that the great Jonah prefigured in his person the foolishness of the Jews. By no means did Jonah himself become subject to any of the proper attributes of the Jews; rather, in his own person he refuted in advance the impiety on account of which the Jews fell away from their former glory, as from a *Joppa* of sorts.

This is why the Holy Spirit mystically conferred on him a name such as Jonah, capable of being translated in different ways so as to demonstrate the peculiar dispositions of all those whom he prefigures. So when he figuratively refutes in his own person the Jews' derangement—a derangement that grieves over the salvation of the Gentiles, is confused over the paradox of the Gentiles' calling, and, blaspheming against the will of God, chooses death and even prefers it over life because the *gourd plant* was withered—Jonah's name is translated "their toil." The text records this when it says, *God saw their works* (clearly referring to the Ninevites), *that they turned from their evil ways; and he repented from doing [bad things] to them, and he did not do them . . . And Jonah was grieved and said, "Now sovereign Lord, take my soul from me, for it is better for me to die than to live . . ."* (Jon 3:10; 4:1, 3); and further, *And the Lord commanded a worm the next morning, and it smote the gourd plant, and it withered away . . . And it happened at [217] sunrise that God summoned a scorching east wind, and the sun smote Jonah's head, and he fainted, and renounced his life, and said, "It is better for me to die than to live"* (Jon 4:7–8).

Nineveh, then, signifies the Church of the Gentiles which, having received the word of grace and turned from its former sin of idolatry, was therefore saved and considered worthy of heavenly glory. The *booth* which Jonah made for himself after he left the city represents the Jerusalem below and the temple built there by human hands (cf Mk 14:58). The *gourd plant* prefigures the transient shadow of the carnal observance of the law in letter alone, which has utterly nothing enduring, nothing capable of enlightening the mind. The *worm* is our Lord and God Jesus Christ, insofar as he says of himself through the prophet David, *I am a worm and not a man* (Ps 21:7, LXX).[11] He truly became, and was thus called, a worm because he assumed the flesh without being conceived by human seed. For, just as the worm is not born through copulation or sexual procreation, so too our Lord was not born in the flesh through sexual procreation. Moreover, the Lord mounted his flesh on the fish-hook of his divinity as bait for the Devil's deceit, so that, as the insatiable spiritual serpent, the Devil would take his flesh into his mouth (since its nature is easily overcome) and quiver convulsively on the hook of the Lord's divinity, and, by virtue of the sacred flesh of the Logos, completely vomit the Lord's human nature once he had swallowed it. As a result, just as the Devil formerly baited man with the hope of divinity, and swallowed him, so too the Devil himself would be baited precisely with humanity's fleshly garb; and afterward he would vomit man, who had been deceived by the expectation of becoming divine, the Devil himself having been deceived by the expectation of becoming human. The transcendence of God's power would then manifest itself through the weakness of our [219] inferior human nature, which would vanquish the strength of its conqueror. As well, it would be shown that it is God who, by using the flesh as bait, conquers the Devil, rather than the Devil conquering man by promising him a divine nature. It is this *worm* who *smote the gourd plant* and caused it to wither—or in other words, who abolished the observance of law like a mere shadow, and dried up the Jews' arrogance over that observance.[12]

[11]Maximus here is following earlier patristic exegetical tradition in interpreting Ps 21:7 christologically and prosopologically (i.e., as a statement uttered by Christ in the person or voice of David).

[12]The analogy of divine deception of the Devil was an ancient one in patristic thought, but the metaphor of the incarnate Logos baiting the Devil by mounting his sacred flesh on the "fish-hook" of his divinity, thus tricking the Devil into releasing captive humanity, has doubtless been picked up by Maximus from Gregory of Nyssa (see *Catechetical Oration* 24, PG 45:64D–65B); it would be used again by John of Damascus (*On the Orthodox Faith* 3.27 (PG 94:1096B–1097A). See also Gustav Aulén, *Christus Victor: An Historical Study of the Three Main Types of the Idea of Atonement,* trans. A. G. Hebert (New York: Macmillan, 1969), pp. 47–55.

And it happened at sunrise the next day . . . (Jon 4:8). On the *next day* because, after surpassing the figurative enigmas of the law and the time dedicated to its carnal observance, the grace of the new mystery arose, bringing about another "day," a day of sublime knowledge and divine virtue, a day able to deify those who seize it. For after this *worm* smote the *gourd plant*, this same *sun* [smote *Jonah*, or the Jews].[13] For he who is the *worm* is also the *Sun of Righteousness* (Mal 3:20, LXX): for one thing, he was born in the flesh without sexual procreation, and his conception was beyond human understanding; for another thing, he went underground, as it were, for my sake, in the mystery of his death and burial, and, existing self-sufficiently by nature like an eternal light, [. . .] he rose from the dead by his resurrection. And *God summoned a scorching east wind, and the sun smote Jonah's head* . . . (Jon 4:8). For after the rising of the *Sun of Righteousness* (that is, the Lord's resurrection and ascension), he who burns up human temptations came upon the Jews who remained impenitent, and smote them on their heads with his righteous judgment, and *turned their toil back onto their own heads,*[14] as Scripture says (Ps 7:17), just as the Jews themselves anticipated when they made a vow against themselves, saying, *His blood be upon us and upon our children* (Mt 27:25). For it is clear that after our Savior's resurrection and ascension, the wind [221] of an exceedingly scorching summer heat appeared, and the vindication of the Gentiles came upon the Jews. Its power smote the power and glory (the *head*, as it were) of every nation, and my *Sun* [*of Righteousness*] overcame it, while the Jews closed their minds' eyes to him, and did not recognize the light of truth that shone on them.

Or from a different perspective,[15] the *wind of a burning heat* stirred up against the Jews who are intransigent toward the word of

---

[13]There is a lacuna in the text at this point, for which we have provided a probable conclusion to Maximus's comparison here.

[14]It should be remembered that Maximus has already designated "their toil" as one of the plausible translations of the name Jonah, bespeaking his prefiguration of the Jewish people.

[15]Frequently in the *Ad Thalassium*, Maximus introduces alternative interpreta-

grace signifies the abandonment which stops the rain of knowledge and the dew of prophecy, and which dries up the natural spring of pious thoughts of the heart. It is an abandonment justly inflicted on people who filled their hands with innocent blood and surrendered truth to falsehood. It is just punishment for people who utterly denied the divine Logos when he came in the form of a human being like us (while still remaining immutable) in order to save the human race; for people who, having denied him, were handed over to the autonomy of delusion, in which there cannot be found, in any form whatsoever, a moral disposition "moistened" by piety and the fear of God, but only a will (γνώμη) that is dry, barren, and shaped to every wicked passion. Pride (τῦφος) alone, an accursed passion composed of the two vices of arrogance (ὑπερηφανία) and vainglory (κενο-δοξία), is able truly to imprint the will.[16] Arrogance denies the Cause of virtue and nature, while vainglory adulterates nature and virtue themselves. The arrogant accomplish nothing godly, and the vainglorious produce nothing natural. Pride is a combination of these two vices. It is contemptuous toward God and accordingly reproaches his providence to the point of blasphemy. Pride is a stranger to nature, and accordingly manipulates everything natural against nature, and in its abusive way distorts the beauty of nature.

In short, the Jewish people, because they did not believe in Christ, were allowed to have their minds bound to the "tempestu-ous" demon of pride, and have thus despised God and humanity equally. [223] On the one hand, the Jews esteem God below carnal pleasure, and thus repudiate worship in the Spirit; on the other hand, they consider those not descended racially from Jacob to be

tions with the phrase ἢ πάλιν, which he have translated "or from a different perspec-tive." He has already indicated above, at the beginning of his response, his predilec-tion for multiple possible (and legitimate) meanings of a single text.

[16]Maximus draws the parallel between the *wind* (Jon 4:8) and "pride" through the etymology of the Greek τῦφος (linked with the Greek mythical figure of Typhon, the father of winds), from which was derived the terms "typhoon" (τυφῶν) and "tem-pestuous" (τυφωνικός) in Greek. Maximus connects this wind with the "euroclydon" (εὐρακύλων), or "typhonic wind" (ἄνεμος τυφωνικός) mentioned in Acts 27:14, as he explains further below in his wordplay on "pride" (τῦφος).

utter aliens to the Creator, and therefore consider their thirst for our blood an object of God's own good pleasure. Most likely, the foolish Jewish people, in their ignorance, did not know that the body is not as capable of relationship with God and familial kinship as the soul, which bears the same mark of faith as all other [faithful] souls, as well as a common internal identity of will in relation to the Good. With this internal identity of will, the law of the flesh is completely done away with, and the Word of God alone is conspicuously manifested through the Spirit, uniting everyone in a common mind in the knowledge of the one God and in a single love for one another and concord. In such a relationship, no one is completely separated spiritually from anyone else, even if, spatially and bodily, they are separated far from each other.

Hence *the wind of a burning heat* is pride, a passion that despises both God and humanity. For in the image of *burning heat*, it dries up the heart of unbelievers, and withers pious thoughts about the Godhead and right principles of created nature. Indeed, they say that this burning heat becomes wind by a mixture of easterly and southerly winds, and thus it dries up the moisture spread over the earth. They say that it is called the "Euroclydon" and "Typhonic" wind (cf Acts 27:14): the Euroclydon because it arouses a tumult from all sides of the earth and sea; the Typhonic because it creates a dusty darkness. Pride (τύφος) has the same effect. For it brings a great tumult upon the soul and fills the mind with the darkness of ignorance. God stirred up this *wind of a burning heat* in the wake of insolence toward Christ; in other words, he allowed that disposition suitable to those who are insolent toward Christ to come upon the Jews, so that their choice respecting God and humanity would become perfectly clear to everyone. [225] Since the Jews were swallowed up in the darkness of ignorance, they willingly drove themselves to the fate of opposing God, and thus have nothing else to do except be troubled and in anguish over the faith-based salvation and glory of the Gentiles, and over the abrogation of their carnal regulations. Thus they say [in the person of Jonah], *Now, Lord, take our lives from us, for it is better for us to die than to live* (Jon 4:3) because of their withered *gourd*—that is, because their observance of the law in shadows was voided, and came and went *before another night* (Jon 4:10) since, in its limitation to symbolic enigmas and types alone, it had no spiritual light that could illumine the soul's thinking.

Let us, however, spiritually embrace, through faith and its concomitant righteousness, the spiritual Nineveh—the Church of the Gentiles, I mean—which is in truth the *great city before God* as it is written (Jon 3:3), and which is preserved by repentance through the *three days* appointed for its conversion. Moreover, let us be zealous to become citizens of this *great city before God* through our own repentance. For the text here quite intentionally mentions that the city before God is *great* when it states that *Nineveh was a great city before God.*

Where in Scripture does the Jew, preoccupied with the earthly city of Jerusalem, find this exact phrase applied thereto? For my part, having read through all of Holy Scripture many times over, I have not found there the phrase *And Jerusalem was a great city before God.* Who would be so confident in his power of reason and in his wealth of ideas as to be able to circumscribe and measure the greatness of the *city before God* that is, and is called, *great.* This would be absolutely impossible for me; yet I suspect that it is also impossible for anyone of intelligence, anyone who [227] has at least a remote sense of the majesty of God; and I am not ignoring the fact that divine determinations must bear a resemblance to God himself.[17] And yet how did the capital of the Assyrians, a city appearing here as the very confusion of sin, under the dominion of the madness of idolatry, a city located so very far from the so-called Holy Land promised to the carnal Israel, come to be a *great city before God,* unless God saw in it the greatness of the faith of the Church of the

---

[17]Having already indicated that the text deliberately specifies the city as *great,* Maximus seems to be suggesting here that the designation is divinely authorized (i.e., its "greatness" is analogous to God's transcendent greatness) and thus cannot apply to the earthly Jerusalem but only to the spiritual Nineveh, the Church of the Gentiles.

Gentiles, a faith no word could fully contain, and, though it was a future faith, accepted it as a present reality, and even dwelled in the foreignness of the city in the meantime? Indeed, through his word God even turned the wretchedness that the city once suffered because of godlessness into the possession of a divine and exalted greatness that no word can define; for as God distinctly said through the prophet, ... *and Nineveh was a great city before God* (Jon 3:3). The word of prophetic grace was sent there and declared a blessed destruction, saying, *Three days still, and Nineveh will be overthrown* (Jon 3:4).

Given that I myself fall within the three-day interval mentioned here, I think that I will pass over other things such as could be stated by those who interpret the text anagogically, and focus with precise observation on one thing alone, and state what will hopefully not be found to stray beyond the truth. Accordingly, when I distinctly hear the prophet proclaiming, *Three days still, and Nineveh will be overthrown*, I expect an unchangeable sentence against Nineveh; but even more precisely, I expect that the visitation will go beyond Nineveh. For I think that after the three days that the prophet spent figuratively in the belly of the whale, by which, in anticipation, he prefigured in his own person the three days of the burial and resurrection of our Lord, the scriptural word anticipated three additional days in which the light of truth and [229] the true fulfillment of foretold mysteries would be revealed, and in which the destruction of the city would be complete. These three days would no longer prefigure the future truth of the Savior's burial and resurrection, but would clearly demonstrate this same truth as realized in actual facts; it was the three days of Jonah's experience in the whale that anticipated this truth and were a prefiguration of it. For if every figure (τύπος) derives from an expected reality (ἀλήθεια), and Jonah spent three days in the whale's belly figuratively, then it is clear that the mystery is going to indicate, in a completely novel way, the truth that follows upon the [original] figure in actual fact, that the Lord has spent three days and three nights in the heart of the earth. The Lord himself attests this when he says, *Just as Jonah was in the belly of the whale three days and three nights, so too the Son of Man will be three days and three nights in the heart of the earth* (Mt 12:40). For the phrase *three days still* (Jon 3:4) signifies that three additional days passed, otherwise the word *still* (ἔτι) would not appear here. In other words, three days were still to transpire and then Nineveh would be destroyed. Thus it was not the figure that destroyed Nineveh according to God's sentence, but the reality, to which the phrase *three days still* refers. It is as if the text were saying that, after the figure already displayed to me, *three days still* of a more mystical burial and a better resurrection shall pass, and Nineveh then shall be destroyed.

Nevertheless, someone still in doubt about this text might very well ask: how is God being truthful when he gives the order for the city's destruction and yet does not destroy it? To such a query we respond that God does in truth both destroy it and save it. [231] He destroys it by causing it to abandon its sin, and he saves it by correcting it with the acquisition of true knowledge; or better yet, he destroys the city's sin with revitalized faith, and brings about its salvation through the death of that sin. For Nineveh is translated "parched blackness" and "smoothest beauty." In harmony with its etymological significance, therefore, the Lord, through his three-day burial and resurrection, destroyed the "parched blackness" of sin that has accrued to human nature through its transgression, and renewed the "smoothest beauty" of that nature through the obedience of faith. He furthermore displayed the "smoothest" beauty of all in human nature, that of the incorruptibility granted through resurrection, a beauty in no way coarsened by materiality. He suited this beauty that I have described to our shared human nature, to the Holy Church, and even to the individual human soul thus ridded through faith and a good conscience of the *earthly image* of the old Adam, and clothed in the *heavenly image* (1 Cor 15:49).

So it has been clearly demonstrated that the prophet Jonah had multifarious spiritual significance attached to him according to the peculiar force of his name, and that each translation of his name is suitably adapted to the contents of the book of Jonah. Translated "flight from beauty," Jonah signifies Adam and our shared human nature. As "healing from God" and "labor of God" he represents our Lord and God according to the exegesis we have provided. He reveals the "grace" of preaching in view of the richness of the Spirit contained therein. He is called "dove," "gift of God," and "labor of God" in view of the many struggles of those who have become servants of the same true calling. Jonah's name is rendered "their toil" since he foreshadows the foolishness of the Jews in resisting the truth, their jealousy of the [233] benefits conferred on foreigners, causing grief for them in their jealousy. Such evil has become second nature for the Jews, who have acquired a hatred of God and humanity alike, and thus they ruthlessly seek only to destroy human nature through bloodshed and murder.

In the course of our exposition, however, we have passed over the spiritual interpretation of the *three-day journey*. For the text reads, *Nineveh was a great city before God, of about a three-day journey* (Jon 3:3). Permit us to fill in this gap with a few observations. We must assume that the *three-day journey* signifies the three different ways of the godly life, or in other words, the discipline proper to each of the three universal laws. By universal laws here I mean the natural law, the scriptural law, and the law of grace. For each of these laws has a peculiar mode of life and appropriate course of action, since each generates a different disposition of the will (γνώμη) for those who follow it. It is only natural that each law creates its own distinct disposition for every one of its subjects.

For example, when the natural law prevents the senses from overpowering reason, it induces all its subjects, without instruction, to embrace those who are of a shared nature and parentage, and to consider their common nature as their instructor for helping those who need it. It induces everyone to desire for everyone else what the individual desires others to do to him. The Lord teaches this when he says, *Whatever you desire for men to do to you, do likewise to them* (Mt 7:12; Lk 6:31). It is only natural for there to be one disposition for those whose human nature is governed by reason; and indeed, not only the same disposition but manifestly the same ethical conduct and [235] way of life. And if their ethical conduct and way of life are the same, they clearly also share the same bond of judgment in their relation to each other, a bond which guides them in single-mindedness toward the one principle of human nature, in which there is absolutely none of the division that possesses human nature because of self-love.

The scriptural law, on the other hand, curbs the unruly urges of the more foolish by the fear of punishment, and trains them to look only for equitable distribution, such that in due time the rule of justice is reinforced and becomes second nature for them, turning their fear (of punishment) into a disposition slowly but surely strengthened by deliberate willing of the good. It turns their customary behavior into a (permanent) habitude purged by the forgetting of their former ways, and simultaneously engenders the love of others. By this love, in turn, the scriptural law reaches its true fulfillment as all human beings are joined to one another in mutual love. For the *fulfillment of the law* (Rom 13:10) consists precisely in the mutual union-in-love of all who share in a common human nature, a union which has charitable desire[18] as the crowning virtue of the rationality of human nature, and which further adorns the law of nature with the addition of that desire. For the law of nature consists in natural reason assuming control of the senses, while the scriptural law, or the fulfillment of the scriptural law, consists in the natural reason acquiring a spiritual desire conducive to a relation of mutuality with others of the same human nature. Therefore the Lord himself specifically says, *Love your neighbor as yourself* (Lev 19:18; Mt 5:43; 19:19; 22:39; Mk 12:31) and not *Regard your neighbor as yourself.* The one indicates only the connatural sharing in being (τὸ εἶναι), while the other signifies the providence leading us toward well-being (τὸ εὖ εἶναι).

---

[18]By "charitable desire" (ὁ κατ' ἀγάπην πόθος), Maximus indicates that human nature's deepest desire, the deepest urges of the soul, must be conformed to, and transformed by, the supreme virtue of godly love.

Finally, the law of grace teaches those who follow it directly to imitate God himself, who, [237] if I may rightly say so, loves us, his virtual enemies because of sin, more than himself, such that, even though he himself transcends every essence and nature, he consented to enter our human essence without undergoing change, and, while retaining his transcendence, to become a man and willingly to interact as one among men. He did not refuse to take our condemnation on himself, and indeed, the more he himself became a man by nature in his incarnation, the more he deified us by grace, so that we would not only learn naturally (φυσικῶς) to care for one another, and spiritually (πνευματικῶς) to love others as ourselves, but also like God (θεϊκῶς) to be concerned for others more than for ourselves, even to the point of proving that love to others by being ready to die voluntarily and virtuously for others. For as the Lord says, *There is no greater love than this, that a man lay down his life for his friend* (Jn 15:13).

In short, then, the law of nature is the natural reason seizing control of the senses in order to rid them of the irrationality from which arises division among human beings who share the same nature. The scriptural law is the natural reason, after it has ridded the senses of irrationality, acquiring a spiritual desire as well, a desire for mutual solidarity with others sharing the same nature. The law of grace consists in a supernatural reason, and transforms nature, without violating it, unto deification. It also displays, beyond comprehension, the supernatural and superessential Archetype in human nature, as in an image, and exhibits the permanence of eternal well-being (τὸ ἀεὶ εὖ εἶναι).[19]

Given our interpretation of the three laws in this way, it is fair to say that the *great city* of God, the Church, or [239] indeed the individual human soul, is a *three-day* journey, insofar as it is receptive of,

[19]In this section we have seen Maximus recall his triad of "being," "well-being," and "eternal well-being" which is central to his teaching on creation, redemption, and deification. Cf *Amb.* 7 (PG 91:1073C, 1084B–C); *Amb.* 42 (1325B–C); also *Ad Thal.* 2 (CCSG 7:51) and *Ad Thal.* 60 (CCSG 22:80).

and fit for, the righteousness of nature, law, and Spirit. For the entire orderly arrangement of the Church is encompassed in these three laws, having its length defined in virtue, its width in knowledge, and its depth in the wisdom of mystical theology.[20]

But let us not, like the Jewish people, be separated in disposition from this city, by loving the body as [Jonah loved his] *booth* (Jon 4:4) and tend to transitory bodily pleasure as [Jonah tended to his] *gourd plant* (Jon 4:6). Otherwise the *worm* of the conscience will smite and wither a disposition deceived by pleasure; and when retribution comes in the form of unsolicited tribulations, like the *wind of a burning heat*, on those of us who have lived in wickedness, we will renounce life and despair over God's judgment. For each of us who has succumbed to the deception of material objects and delighted in bodily pleasure is all the while receiving the word of God like a *worm* smiting him in his conscience, and devouring his attachment to pleasure like the root of the *gourd plant*. So too the word of God dries up the activity of sin with the rising sunlight of the oracles of the Spirit (cf Jon 4:8), and, by recalling the threat of eternal punishment, like the *wind of a burning heat*, smites—as though it were the sinner's *head*—the source of depraved passions amid the provocations of the senses. The word of God does all of this so that we will learn the principles of God's providence and judgment, which give priority to eternal realities over transitory things, the deprivation of which habitually causes grief for the human race.

For if the word of Scripture represents man as grieving over his *booth* and his *gourd plant* (that is, over the flesh and carnal pleasure), but represents God as caring for *Nineveh*, then it is clear that whatever appears to be dear to God is so much better and more honorable that any existent thing precious to man, much less anything

---

[20]This triad of virtue, knowledge, and mystical theology evokes the three dimensions of the spiritual life—ascetic practice (πρᾶξις), contemplation (θεωρία), and mystical theology (θεολογία)—which Maximus appropriated from Evagrius and expounded abundantly in his spiritual writings. See Thunberg, *Microcosm and Mediator*, pp. 332–68.

non-existent, which seems to exist merely by the presumption of mistaken judgment when actually it has no existential basis at all; indeed, mere fantasy deceives the mind and, through passion, causes vain attachment to objects that do not exist, but provides no foundation in reality.[21]

[21]Here as elsewhere, Maximus presupposes the principle of the "non-existence" of evil objects of human infatuation. Beginning with Adam, humanity has been deceived by merely *apparent* goods, which, ontologically speaking, do not participate in the true Good and thus do not truly exist. They "exist" only in human fantasy and attendant passions and sinful acts. Cf Gregory of Nyssa's famous dictum that man "invented" evil (*De virginitate* 12, GNO 8, pt. 1: 298, 21–299, 12), thus giving it a relative "existence" though it holds no genuine ontological status in God's creation.

OPUSCULUM 6

On the Two Wills of Christ in the Agony of Gethsemane

(PG 91:65A–68D)

[65A] If you understand Jesus's prayer, *Father, if possible, let* [65B] *this cup pass from me* (Mt 26:39), which gives the indication of resistance (συστολή), as expressed by the man "not that we conceive in the role of Savior (for his will in no way contradicts God, since it has been completely deified), but who is just like us, seeing as the human will does not always follow God but so often resists and contends with him," as the divine Gregory says,[1] what do you make of the rest of the prayer, *Let not what I will, but what you will prevail*? Is it a matter of resistance (συστολή) or courage (ἀνδρεία), of agreement (σύννευσις) or disagreement (διάστασις)? Certainly no one of a right mind will dispute that it is a matter neither of contention (ἀντίπτωσις) nor cowardice (δειλία) but of perfect harmony (συμφυΐα) and concurrence (σύννευσις).[2]

---

[1]Gregory Nazianzen, *Oration* 30.12, Greek text ed. Paul Gallay, *Grégoire de Nazianze, Discours 27–31 (Discours théologiques)*, SC 250 (Paris: Cerf, 1978), pp. 248, 5–250, 1.

[2]The stakes of linguistic precision in this text are extraordinarily high, thus Maximus's meticulous use of terms. See the extensive discussion of this text and its wider background in Léthel, *Théologie de l'agonie du Christ*, especially pp. 29–49, 86–99; also Piret, *Le Christ et la Trinité*, pp. 247–63. As Léthel has shown, the dilemma before Maximus in this opuscule is the emerging Monotheletism advanced in the *Psephos*, a document issued by Patriarch Sergius of Constantinople in June of 633. Sergius doubtless hoped to exploit Gregory Nazianzen's comments from *Or.* 30.12, quoted only in part

...nd if it is a matter of perfect harmony and concurrence, whom do you [65C] understand as the subject? The man who is just like us, or the man we consider in the role of Savior? If it is from the man who is just like us, then our teacher Gregory errs when he declares "... seeing as the human will does not always follow God but so often resists and contends with him." For if it follows God, it is not resisting him, and if it is resisting him, it is not following him. These two assertions, being contrary, mutually nullify [68A] and exclude each other. If, however, you understand the subject of the phrase *Let not what I will, but what you will prevail* to be not the man just like us but the man we consider as Savior, then you have confessed the ultimate concurrence of his human will with the divine will, which is both his and the Father's; and you have demonstrated that with the duality of his natures there are two wills (θελήσεις) and two operations (ἐνεργείαι) respective to the two natures, and that he admits of no opposition between them, even though he maintains all the while the difference between the two natures from which, in which, and which he is by nature.[3]

here by Maximus. Nazianzen actually had made this statement while trying to explain the words of Jesus's Gethsemane prayer in a properly *trinitarian* (anti-Arian) rather than christological context. He took Jesus's words in Jn 6:38 ("for I have come down from heaven, not to do my own will, but the will of him who sent me") as definitive also for his prayer in Gethsemane. The subject of these statements is *not* the man Jesus, but the Son of God, whose negation of having his own will positively affirms the absence of a separate (= contrary) will from the Father's proper to his hypostasis. Sergius inferred from this the absence of a separate (= contrary) *human* will in Christ as well. Now Maximus, interpreting both the Gethsemane prayer and Nazianzen's comments in a distinctly *christological* register, and keen to recover the integrity and salvific importance of Christ's human will, follows a quite different logic. The subject of the prayer is precisely the man who is at once "like us" in the possession of a natural human will *and* him "whom we conceive in the role of Savior" insofar as his human will has already been assumed within the mode (τρόπος) of the hypostatic union. Maximus explains this more explicitly in *Opusc.* 3 (PG 91:48C–D).

[3]ἐξ ὧν καὶ ἐν αἷς τε, καὶ ἅπερ ἦν ὁ αὐτὸς κατὰ φύσιν. This important description of Christ's person (ὑπόστασις) being not only composed *from* and *in* the two natures, divine and human, but also existing *as* those two natures, represents Maximus's concern to work out the full implications of the Chalcedonian Definition. This formulation appears elsewhere in Maximus's works: *Amb.* 27 (PG 91:1269C); ibid. 5, (1052D); *Epistle* 15 (PG 91:573A); ibid. 12 (488C); *Opusc.* 7 (PG 91:80C); ibid. 19

But if, constrained by these arguments, you proceed to say that the negation *Not* [68B] *what I will* comes neither from the man who is just like us, nor from the man whom we consider in the role of Savior, but rather refers, as a negation, to the eternal divinity of the Only-Begotten—which [*ipso facto*] excludes his willing something for himself separately from the Father—then you are compelled to refer what is willed, which is precisely the declining of the cup, to the very same eternal divinity. For even if you say that the negation is the negation of his willing something for himself separately from his Father, it is nevertheless not a dismissal of what is willed itself. For it is impossible for the negation to apply to both things: the Only-Begotten's willing something for himself separately from the Father *and* that which is willed itself. Otherwise, since the Father and the Son always share a common will, negation would be negation of what is willed by God, namely, our salvation—and we know that is what God wills by his very nature. But if it is impossible for the negation to apply to both things mentioned above, it is obvious that if you opt to apply it to the Son willing something for himself, in order to affirm the common [68C] will between Father and Son, you are not repudiating what is willed, namely, the declining of the cup, but you are in fact ascribing that declining to their common and eternal divinity, to which you have also referred the exercise of will in the negating.

(224A); ibid. 1 (36C). For a complete survey of its significance in Maximus, see Pierre Piret, *Le Christ et la Trinité selon Maxime le Confesseur*, Théologie historique 69 (Paris: Beauchesne, 1983), 203–39. Piret argues that Maximus adopted from Cyril of Alexandria the notion of Christ being composed "from" (ἐκ) the two natures; and he of course derived the phrase "in" (ἐν) two natures from the Chalcedonian Definition; but the assertion that Christ's person *is* the two natures was uniquely his own (p. 204). Yet Demetrios Bathrellos has shown that in this identification of Christ's person *as* the two natures, Maximus is following a formula already in Leontius of Byzantium (PG 86:1904A). Christ *is* the two natures, however, not in the sense that the natures are purely collapsible or reducible to the one hypostasis. It is a properly and perfectly irreducible relationship between his person and natures ("ΧΡΙΣΤΟΣ ΘΕΛΩΝ: Person, Nature and Will in Ancient Christology with Special Reference to Saint Maximus the Confessor" [Ph.D. dissertation, Kings College, University of London, 2000], pp. 124–25 and notes 49–50).

Now if even the thought of such reasoning is repugnant, then clearly the negation here—*Not what I will*—absolutely precludes opposition and instead demonstrates harmony between the human will of the Savior and the divine will shared by him and his Father, given that the Logos assumed our nature in its entirety and deified his human will in the assumption. It follows, then, that having become like us for our sake, he was calling on his God and Father in a human manner (ἀνθρωποπρεπῶς) when he said, *Let not what I will, but what you will prevail,* inasmuch as, being God by nature, he also in his humanity has, as his human volition, the fulfillment of the will of the Father.[4] This is why, considering both of the natures from which, [68D] in which, and of which his person was, he is acknowledged as able both to will and to effect our salvation. As God, he approved that salvation along with the Father and the Holy Spirit; as man, he *became* for the sake of that salvation *obedient* to his Father *unto death, even death on a cross* (Phil 2:8). He accomplished this great feat of the economy of salvation for our sake through the mystery of his incarnation.

---

[4]Elsewhere Maximus explains in more depth the element of "resistance" in Christ's Gethsemane prayer. He renders the apparent "resistance" transparent to a deeper economy in which Christ is graciously transforming human passions like the fear of death. See already *Ad Thal.* 21 (CCSG 7:131, 80–85; and above, pp. 112–3 and note 7). In the *Disputation with Pyrrhus* (PG 91:297B), for example, he speaks of Christ's blameless "use" of this fear for our sake, while in *Opusc.* 3 (PG 91:48C–D) and *Opusc.* 7 (80C–D) he affirms Christ's fear of death, a sign of his true humanity, as integral to his voluntary submission to the will of the Father, aimed ultimately at modeling self-abnegation and emboldening those who confront death on the basis of their obedience.

Select Bibliography

PRIMARY SOURCES USED IN THIS TRANSLATION

Maximi Confessoris Quaestiones ad Thalassium. I. *Quaestiones I-LV una cum latine interpretatione Ioannis Scotti Eriugenae.* Edited by Carl Laga and Carlos Steel. Corpus christianorum, series graeca (CCSG) 7. Turnhout: Brepols / Leuven University Press, 1980.

Maximi Confessoris Quaestiones ad Thalassium. II. *Quaestiones LVI-LXV una cum latine interpretatione Ioannis Scotti Eriugenae.* Edited by Carl Laga and Carlos Steel. Corpus christianorum, series graeca (CCSG) 22. Turnhout: Brepols / Leuven University Press, 1990.

Maximus the Confessor. *Liber ambiguorum (Ambigua).* Patrologia graeca (PG), vol. 91, columns 1031–1418 (Paris: J.-P. Migne, 1865).

Maximus the Confessor. *Opuscula theologica et polemica.* Patrologia graeca (PG), vol. 91, columns 10–286. (Paris: J.-P. Migne, 1865).

ADDITIONAL PRIMARY SOURCES AND TRANSLATIONS

Allen, Pauline, and Bronwen Neil, editors. *Documenta ad vitam sancti Maximi Confessoris spectantia,* Corpus christianorum, series graeca. Leuven: Brepols, forthcoming.

Allen, Pauline, and Bronwen Neil, editors. *Scripta saeculi VII vitam Maximi Confessoris illustrantia,* Corpus christianorum, series graeca, vol. 39. Turnhout: Brepols, 1999.

Allen, Pauline, and Bronwen Neil, editors and translators. *Maximus the Confessor and His Companions: Documents from Exile,* Oxford Early Christian Texts. Oxford: Oxford University Press, 2002.

Berthold, George, editor and translator. *Maximus Confessor: Selected Writings.* Classics of Western Spirituality. Mahwah, N.J.: Paulist Press, 1985.

Birchall, Christopher, translator. *The Life of Our Holy Father Maximus the Confessor*. Boston: Holy Transfiguration Monastery, 1982.

Congourdeau, Marie-Hélène, editor and translator. *Maxime le Confesseur: L'agonie du Christ.* Introduction by François-Marie Léthel. Les pères dans la foi. Paris: Migne, 1996. (= French translation of Maximus's christological *Opuscula*)

Sherwood, Polycarp, translator. *St. Maximus the Confessor: The Ascetic Life and Four Centuries on Charity*. Ancient Christian Writers 21. Westminster, Md.: Newman Press, 1957.

SECONDARY STUDIES

Balthasar, Hans Urs von. *Kosmische Liturgie: Das Weltbild Maximus' des Bekenners*. 2nd edition. Einsiedeln: Johannes-Verlag, 1961.

Bathrellos, Demetrios. "ΧΡΙΣΤΟΣ ΘΕΛΩΝ: Person, Nature and Will in Ancient Christology with Special Reference to Saint Maximus the Confessor." Ph.D. dissertation, Kings College, University of London, 2000.

Bausenhart, Guido. *In Allem uns gleich ausser der Sunde: Studien zum Beitrag Maximos' des Bekenners zur altchristlichen Christologie*. Tübinger Studien zur Theologie und Philosophie 5. Mainz: Matthias Grünewald, 1995.

Berthold, George. "The Cappadocian Roots of Maximus the Confessor." In *Maximus Confessor: Actes du symposium sur Maxime le Confesseur, Fribourg, 2–5 septembre 1980*, pp. 51–9. Edited by Felix Heinzer and Christoph Schönborn. Paradosis 27. Fribourg: Éditions Universitaires, 1982.

Blowers, Paul M. *Exegesis and Spiritual Pedagogy in Maximus the Confessor: An Investigation of the "Quaestiones ad Thalassium."* Christianity and Judaism in Antiquity 7. Notre Dame, Ind.: University of Notre Dame Press, 1991.

Blowers, Paul M. "Gentiles of the Soul: Maximus the Confessor on the Substructure and Transformation of the Human Passions." *Journal of Early Christian Studies* 4 (1996): 57–85.

Blowers, Paul M. "Maximus the Confessor, Gregory of Nyssa, and the Concept of 'Perpetual Progress.'" *Vigiliae Christianae* 46 (1992): 151–71.

Blowers, Paul M. "The Passion of Jesus Christ in Maximus the Confessor: A

Reconsideration." *Studia Patristica* 37, pp. 361–77. Edited by M. F. Wiles and E. J. Yarnold. Leuven: Peeters Press, 2001.

Blowers, Paul M. "Realized Eschatology in Maximus the Confessor, *Ad Thalassium* 22." *Studia Patristica* 32, pp. 258–63. Edited by Elizabeth Livingstone. Leuven: Peeters Press, 1997.

Blowers, Paul M. "Theology as Visionary, Integrative, Pastoral: The Legacy of Maximus the Confessor." *Pro Ecclesia* 2 (1993): 216–30.

Blowers, Paul M. "The World in the Mirror of Holy Scripture: Maximus the Confessor's Short Hermeneutical Treatise in *Ambiguum ad Joannem* 37." In *In Dominico Eloquio—In Lordly Eloquence: Essays on Patristic Exegesis in Honor of Robert Louis Wilken*, pp. 408–26. Edited by Paul M. Blowers, Angela Russell Christman, David G. Hunter, and Robin Darling Young. Grand Rapids: Eerdmans, 2002.

Boojamra, John. "Original Sin according to St. Maximus the Confessor." *St Vladimir's Theological Quarterly* 20 (1976): 19–30.

Brock, Sebastian. "An Early Syriac Life of Maximus the Confessor." *Analecta Bollandiana* 91 (1975): 299–346.

Cameron, Averil. *Changing Cultures in Early Byzantium*. Variorum Collected Studies 536. Aldershot, U.K. and Brookfield, Vt.: Variorum, 1996.

Cooper, Adam. "Holy Flesh, Wholly Deified: The Place of the Body in the Theological Vision of Saint Maximus the Confessor." Ph.D. dissertation, University of Durham, 2002.

Cooper, Adam. "Maximus the Confessor and the Structural Dynamics of Revelation." *Vigiliae Christianae* 55 (2001): 161–86.

Croce, Vittorio. *Tradizione e ricerca: Il metodo teologico di san Massimo il Confessore*. Studia patristica mediolanensia 2. Milan: Vita e Pensiero, 1974.

Dalmais, Irénée-Henri. "L'anthropologie spirituelle de saint Maxime le Confesseur." *Recherches et débats* 36 (1961): 202–11.

Dalmais, Irénée-Henri. "La fonction unificatrice du Verbe Incarné dans les oeuvres spirituelles de saint Maxime le Confesseur." *Sciences ecclésiastiques* 14 (1962): 445–59.

Dalmais, Irénée-Henri. "La manifestation du Logos dans l'homme et dans l'Église: Typologie anthropologique et typologie écclesiale d'après Qu. Thal. 60 et la Mystagogie." In *Maximus Confessor: Actes du symposium sur Maxime le Confesseur, Fribourg, 2–5 septembre 1980*, pp. 13–25. Edited by Felix Heinzer and Christoph Schönborn. Paradosis 27. Fribourg: Éditions Universitaires, 1982.

Dalmais, Irénée-Henri. "La théorie des 'logoi' des créatures chez saint
Maxime le Confesseur." *Revue des sciences philosophiques et théologiques*
36 (1952): 244–49.

Dalmais, Irénée-Henri. "Saint Maxime Confesseur et la crise de l'origénisme
monastique." In *Théologie de la vie monastique: études sur la tradition
patristique*, pp. 411–21. Théologie 49. Paris: Aubier, 1961.

Doucet, Marcel. "La volonté humaine du Christ, spécialment en son agonie:
Maxime le Confesseur, interprète de l'Écriture." *Science et esprit* 37
(1985): 123–59.

Draeseke, J. "Zu Maximus Confessor." *Zeitschrift für wissenschaftliche Theologie* 47 (1904): 250–59.

Duval, Yves-Marie. *Le livre de Jonas dans la littérature chrétienne grecque et
latine*, 2 vols. Paris: Études Augustiniennes, 1973.

Florovsky, Georges. *The Byzantine Fathers of the Sixth to Eighth Century.*
Collected Works of Georges Florovsky 9. Translated by Raymond
Miller, Anne-Marie Döllinger-Labriolle, and Helmut Schmiedel. Vaduz:
Büchervertriebsanstalt, 1987.

Garrigues, Juan-Miguel. *Maxime le Confesseur: La charité, avenir divin de
l'homme.* Théologie historique 38. Paris: Beauchesne, 1976.

Haldon, John. *Byzantium in the Seventh Century: The Transformation of a
Culture.* Cambridge: Cambridge University Press, 1990.

Heinzer, Felix. *Gottes Sohn als Mensch: Die Struktur des Menschseins Christi
bei Maximus Confessor.* Paradosis 16. Fribourg: Éditions Universitaires,
1980.

Heinzer, Felix. "L'explication trinitaire de l'économie chez Maxime le Confesseur." In *Maximus Confessor: Actes du symposium sur Maxime le Confesseur, Fribourg, 2–5 septembre 1980*, pp. 160–72. Edited by Felix Heinzer
and Christoph Schönborn. Paradosis 27. Fribourg: Éditions Universitaires, 1982.

Karayiannis, Vasilios. *Maxime le Confesseur: essence et energies de Dieu.*
Théologie historique 93. Paris: Beauchesne, 1993.

Laga, Carl. "Maximi Confessoris *ad Thalassium Quaestio* 64." In *After Chalcedon: Studies in Theology and Church History Offered to Professor Albert
Van Roey for His Seventieth Birthday*, pp. 203–15. Edited by Carl Laga,
J.A. Munitz, and L. van Rompay. Orientalia lovaniensia analecta 18. Leuven: Departement Oriëntalistiek, 1985.

Larchet, Jean-Claude. "Ancestral Guilt according to St. Maximus the Confessor: A Bridge between Eastern and Western Conceptions." *Sobornost* 20 (1998): 26–48 (= English translation of chapter 2 of his *Maxime le Confesseur, médiateur entre l'Orient et l'Occident*).

Larchet, Jean-Claude. "Le baptême selon Maxime le Confesseur." *Revue des sciences religieuses* 65 (1991): 51–70.

Larchet, Jean-Claude. *La divinisation de l'homme selon saint Maxime le Confesseur*. Cogitatio fidei 194. Paris: Les Éditions du Cerf, 1996.

Larchet, Jean-Claude. *Maxime le Confesseur, médiateur entre l'Orient et l'Occident*. Cogitatio Fidei 208. Paris: Les Éditions du Cerf, 1998.

Léthel, François-Marie. *Théologie de l'agonie du Christ: la liberté humaine du Fils de Dieu et son importance sotériologique mises en lumière par saint Maxime le Confesseur*. Théologie historique 52. Paris: Beauchesne, 1979.

Louth, Andrew. *Maximus the Confessor*. The Early Church Fathers. London and New York: Routledge, 1996 (includes English translation of select texts of Maximus).

Louth, Andrew. "Recent Research on St. Maximus the Confessor: A Survey." *St Vladimir's Theological Quarterly* 42 (1998): 67–84.

Louth, Andrew. "St. Denys the Areopagite and St. Maximus the Confessor: A Question of Influence." *Studia Patristica* 27, pp. 166–74. Edited by Elizabeth Livingstone. Leuven: Peeters Press, 1993.

Louth, Andrew. "St. Maximus the Confessor: Between East and West." *Studia Patristica* 32, pp. 332–45. Edited by Elizabeth Livingstone. Leuven: Peeters Press, 1997.

Louth, Andrew. *Wisdom of the Byzantine Church: Evagrios of Pontos and Maximos the Confessor*. 1997 Paine Lectures in Religion, University of Missouri. Columbia: University of Missouri, 1998.

McGuckin, John. *St. Cyril of Alexandria: The Christological Controversy: Its History, Theology, and Texts*. Supplements to *Vigiliae Christianae* 23. Leiden: E. J. Brill, 1994.

McGuckin, John. *Saint Gregory of Nazianzus: An Intellectual Biography*. Crestwood, N.Y.: St Vladimir's Seminary Press, 2001.

Meyendorff, John. *Christ in Eastern Christian Thought*. Crestwood, N.Y.: St Vladimir's Seminary Press, 1975 (especially chapter 7, "The Cosmic Dimension of Salvation," on St. Maximus).

Miquel, Pierre. "Πεῖρα: Contribution à l'étude du vocabulaire de l'expérience religieuse dans l'oeuvre de Maxime le Confesseur," *Studia Patristica* 7, pp. 355–61. Berlin: Akademie-Verlag, 1966.

Nellas, Panayiotis. *Deification in Christ: Orthodox Perspectives on the Nature of the Human Person.* Translated by Norman Russell. Crestwood, N.Y.: St Vladimir's Seminary Press, 1987.

Nichols, Aidan. *Byzantine Gospel: Maximus the Confessor in Recent Scholarship.* Edinburgh: T & T Clark, 1996.

O'Regan, Cyril. "Von Balthasar and Thick Retrieval: Post-Chalcedonian Symphonic Theology." *Gregorianum* 77 (1996): 227–60.

Pelikan, Jaroslav. " 'Council or Father or Scripture': The Concept of Authority in the Theology of Maximus the Confessor." In *The Heritage of the Early Church: Essays in Honor of Georges Florovsky,* pp. 277–88. Edited by David Neiman and Margaret Schatkin. Orientalia christiana analecta 195. Rome: Pontifical Institute of Oriental Studies, 1973.

Piret, Pierre. *Le Christ et la Trinité selon Maxime le Confesseur.* Théologie historique 69. Paris: Beauchesne, 1983.

Prado, José J. *Voluntad y naturaleza: La antropología filosófica de Maximo el Confesor.* Rio Cuarto, Argentina: Ediciónes de la Universidad Nacional de Rio Cuarto, 1974.

Riou, Alain. *Le monde et l'Église selon Maxime le Confesseur.* Théologie historique 22. Paris: Beauchesne, 1973.

Schönborn, Christoph. "Plaisir et douleur dans l'analyse de S. Maxime, d'après les *Quaestiones ad Thalassium.*" In *Maximus Confessor: Actes du Symposium sur Maxime le Confesseur, Fribourg, 2–5 septembre 1980,* pp. 273–84. Edited by Felix Heinzer and Christoph Schönborn. Paradosis 27. Fribourg: Éditions Universitaires, 1982).

Sherwood, Polycarp. *An Annotated Date-List of the Works of Maximus the Confessor.* Studia anselmiana 30. Rome: Herder, 1952.

Sherwood, Polycarp. *The Earlier Ambigua of St. Maximus the Confessor and His Refutation of Origenism.* Studia anselmiana 36. Rome: Herder, 1955.

Sherwood, Polycarp. "Maximus and Origenism: ΑΡΧΗ ΚΑΙ ΤΕΛΟΣ." *Berichte zum XI. internationalen Byzantinisten-Kongress* III, 1, pp. 1–27. Münich, 1958.

Staniloae, Dumitru. "Commentaires" on the *Ambigua* of St. Maximus, French translation from the Romanian by Père Aurel Grigoras. Appended to *Saint Maxime le Confesseur: Ambigua,* French translation by Emmanuel Ponsoye, pp. 373–540. Paris and Suresnes: Les Éditions de l'Ancre, 1994.

Telepneff, Gregory, and Bishop Chrysostomos. "The Person, *Pathe*, Asceticism, and Spiritual Restoration in Saint Maximos." *Greek Orthodox Theological Review* 34 (1989): 249–61.

Thunberg, Lars. *Man and the Cosmos: The Vision of St Maximus the Confessor*. Crestwood, N.Y.: St Vladimir's Seminary Press, 1985.

Thunberg, Lars. *Microcosm and Mediator: The Theological Anthropology of Maximus the Confessor*. 2nd edition. Chicago: Open Court Publishing, 1995.

Tollefsen, Torstein. *The Christocentric Cosmology of St. Maximus the Confessor: A Study of His Metaphysical Principles*, Acta Humaniora 72. Oslo: Unipub Forlag, 2000.

Völker, Walther. *Maximus Confessor als Meister des geistlichen Lebens*. Wiesbaden: Franz Steiner, 1965.

Wilken, Robert L. "Maximus the Confessor on the Affections in Historical Perspective." In *Asceticism*, pp. 412–23. Edited by Vincent Wimbush and Richard Valantasis, New York: Oxford University Press.

Yeago, David. "Jesus of Nazareth and Cosmic Redemption: The Relevance of St. Maximus the Confessor." *Modern Theology* 12 (1996): 163–93.

Zirnheld, Claire-Agnès. "Le double visage de la passion: malédiction due au péché et/ou dynamisme de la vie: *Quaestiones ad Thalassium* XXI, XXII et XLII." In *Philohistôr: miscellanea in honorem Caroli Laga septuagenarii*. Orientalia lovaniensia analecta 60, pp. 361–80. Edited by A. Schoors and P. van Deun. Leuven: Peeters Press, 1994.

Index of Biblical References

POPULAR PATRISTICS SERIES

ST VLADIMIR'S SEMINARY PRESS
1-800-204-2665 • www.svspress.com